T0311755

KARL ABRAHAM

KARL ABRAHAM

At the Roots of
Analytic Theory

Franco De Masi

Routledge
Taylor & Francis Group

LONDON AND NEW YORK

Originally published in Italian in 2002 by
Armando Editore as
Karl Abraham: Alle radici della teoria analitica

Translated by Janice Parker

First published 2018
by Routledge
2 Park Square, Milton Park, Abingdon, Oxon OX14 4RN

and by Routledge
711 Third Avenue, New York, NY 10017

Routledge is an imprint of the Taylor & Francis Group, an informa business

British Library Cataloguing-in-Publication Data
A catalogue record for this book is available from the British Library

Library of Congress Cataloging-in-Publication Data
A catalog record has been requested for this book

ISBN: 9781782205128 (pbk)

Typeset in Palatino
by The Studio Publishing Services Ltd
www.publishingservicesuk.co.uk
email: studio@publishingservicesuk.co.uk

CONTENTS

ABOUT THE AUTHOR

Franco De Masi is a member of the Italian Psychoanalytic Society, and a former President of the Centro Milanese di Psicoanalisi and Secretary of the Training Institute of Milan. He is a medical doctor and psychiatrist who worked for many years in psychiatric hospitals, and has for the past thirty-five years worked as a full-time psychoanalyst in Milan. Theoretical and technical psychoanalytic issues related to severely ill or psychotic patients are where his main interests lie.

Dr De Masi has written psychoanalytic papers published in the *Italian Psychoanalytic Annual* (*Rivista Italiana di Psicoanalisi*) and the *International Journal of Psychoanalysis*. He is the author of *The Sadomasochistic Perversion: The Entity and the Theories*, Karnac (2003); *Making Death Thinkable: A Psychoanalytic Contribution to the Problem of the Transience of Life*, Free Association Books (2004); *Vulnerability to Psychosis*, Karnac (2009); *The Enigma of Suicide Terrorism*, Karnac (2011); *Working with Difficult Patients*, Karnac (2015); and has also edited the book *Herbert Rosenfeld at Work. The Italian Seminars* (2001), published by Karnac.

Introduction

The life of Karl Abraham, ending prematurely when he was forty-eight years of age, is outlined in this short book that also charts the fundamental contribution he made to psychoanalytic clinical theory and describes in depth the important bond he had with Freud. Not only was Abraham Freud's most loyal companion following the break with Jung, but he was also a close friend in what was a reciprocally enriching relationship. A man of great mental poise and one of the few followers who did not undergo analysis, Abraham was, on more than one occasion, able to discern, even before Freud himself, various crises in the making within the psychoanalytic group.

His premature death came at a considerable cost to the psycho-analytic movement. Abraham was President of the International Association, he was accorded a certain prestige, and his Berlin school attracted extremely promising young analysts. He was also a co-founder of the Berlin Polyclinic, and the training method he devised went on to be adopted by all psychoanalytic societies.

His passing away left the movement without an undisputed leader. Had Abraham, backed by Freud, been able to take over the leadership of the movement, it is most unlikely that the irreconcilable conflict between Anna Freud and Melanie Klein would have come to a head.

Over the years, his scientific works have continued to form the base of analytic clinical practice: the transference, narcissism, envy, and the importance of the infantile emotional trauma, for example, not to mention his three important essays on melancholic depression. Beyond these three essays, his examination of melancholy comes through in the all-important correspondence between himself and Freud, which, in my view, out of all similar correspondence that has been published, is the most fruitful from a scientific viewpoint. An example of authentic analytic dialogue, Freud and Abraham's correspondence contains creative thought and shows the development of valuable analytic intuitions: first comes a question from Abraham, who is keen to understand, next, Freud's enlightening and balanced reply that always leaves the way open for his interlocutor's response, then the pupil's quick insight and further, more exact, observations that lead to yet other formulations.

Melancholy is the subject that both were particularly interested in and about which they exchanged their respective thoughts. Several of Abraham's ideas tie in with those in Freud's "Mourning and melancholia", both men, I believe, having fully highlighted the origin and dynamics of this mental state. I have sought to bring out this joint effort of theirs, and Abraham's contribution in particular, which sheds light on the importance of recreating a lost object in one's internal world, a subject that Melanie Klein then went on to develop.

Differences between Abraham and Klein have also been underlined. For instance, Klein's assertion that she had drawn on Abraham's theoretical contribution when formulating her theory (especially with regard to destructiveness as the original drive) is not quite the case. It is worth noting, regardless of the fact that he died only four years after the publication of Freud's essay *Beyond the Pleasure Principle* (1920g), that Abraham had on no occasion mentioned the death drive, but was faithful to the view that aggressiveness derived from the original trauma. An example of these dynamics is his wonderful essay on the artist Segantini.

Original in Abraham's thinking with respect to Freud's is the greater value he gave to the bond with the mother as opposed to the father. As far back as 1909, Abraham asked Freud in a letter whether he was still convinced that the father was more important to the child's development than the mother. The gap between them concerning the importance of the conflict with the mother and the secondary role played by the father was, indeed, substantial. Abraham, for instance, attributed to the mother the origin of the affective trauma out of which the object relation of melancholy develops. Painfully rejected by his mother, Segantini's response was one of hatred and death wishes against her, and overriding was the trauma of abandonment.

In brief, as well as informing the reader of Abraham's contribution to analytic theory and clinical work, this short book has sought to bring out Abraham's original thinking, both in general and in relation to his master, Freud, and pupil, Melanie Klein.

We are like dwarves perched on the shoulders of giants, and thus we are able to see more and farther than the latter. And this is not at all because of the acuteness of our sight or the stature of our body, but because we are carried aloft and elevated by the magnitude of the giants. (Bernard of Chartres)

CHAPTER ONE

His life

On December 25, 1925, Dr Karl Abraham, President and founder of the Berlin Psycho-Analytical Society and President for the time being of the International Psycho-Analytical Association, died in Berlin. He had not yet reached the age of fifty years when he succumbed to an illness against which his vigorous physique had been struggling ever since the early summer. At the Congress at Homburg his apparent recovery delighted us all; but to our grievous disappointment there followed a relapse.

We bury with him—integer vitae scelerisque purus—one of the surest hopes we had for our science, young as it is and still so bitterly assailed, and a part of its future which will now, perhaps, never come to fruition. So high a place had he won for himself that, of all who have followed me through the dark pathways of psycho-analytic research, there is only one whose name could be put beside his.[1] Colleagues and younger workers had an unbounded faith in him, so that it is likely that the leadership would have been his. And indeed, he would have been a model leader in the pursuit of truth, led astray neither by the praise and blame of the many nor by the tempting illusion of his own phantasies.

I am writing these lines for friends and fellow-workers who knew and valued him as I did. They will easily understand what the loss of this friend, who was so much younger than myself, means to me, and they will forgive me if I make no further attempt to express things for which it is hard to find words.

This is how, in the first issue of the *International Journal of Psychoanalysis*, shortly after Abraham's death, Freud conveyed his grief for the loss of his friend and colleague from Berlin.

At the beginning of 1925, Abraham had fallen ill with an infectious disease diagnosed as aspiration pneumonia. His doctors were unable to understand the cause of what seemed to be a lung abscess and the infection turned out to be so severe that every therapy failed. Abraham remained hopeful about recovery but Freud's worry deepened. Then, in October, Abraham wrote of complications: a swollen and painful liver. Convinced that he was suffering from a gall-bladder complaint, Abraham insisted on surgery.[2]

Freud's concern nevertheless persisted: in the light of a retrospective diagnosis, Abraham's illness turned out to be none other than cancer which had clinically manifested as a lung abscess.

Abraham died on Christmas Day, 1925. The news of Abraham's death reached Freud immediately. That same day he wrote the short obituary shown above, while Ernest Jones undertook to outline the biography and scientific contribution of their deceased colleague.

On 30th December, Freud wrote to Jones,

Abraham's death is perhaps the greatest loss that could have hit us, and it has hit us. In letters I jokingly called him my *rocher de bronze*; I felt safe in the absolute confidence he inspired in me, as in everyone else. . . . Who would have thought, when we met that time in the Harz, that he would be the first to leave this irrational life. We must work on and keep together. No one can personally replace our loss, but then for our work, no one can be indispensable. I shall soon pass on, others not till much later, I hope, but our work, compared to whose importance we are all insignificant, must continue. (Paskauskas, 1993, p. xxxv)

And then, in a letter to Pfister on 3rd January 1926, Freud wrote,

With us the situation, not to say the whole atmosphere, is dominated by Abraham's death which, as you know, took place on Christmas Day. He is a great loss to us, and he will hardly be replaceable. I write this refraining from all emotional reactions and assessing his objective value only. (Freud & Pfister, 1963, p. 101)

Who was Abraham and what did he represent within the international psychoanalytic movement? Why was he so well thought of and what made him so important as to be elected President of the International Psychoanalytical Association? What did he bring to the collaboration with Freud that made him irreplaceable and mourned with such sorrow? Was his unique approach to research really on a par with his personal attributes and his ability to organise and lead the psychoanalytic movement?

Karl Abraham was born in Bremen on 3rd May 1877, the second of two boys born into a strictly orthodox Jewish family. The family home was large and shared with many other relatives: besides Karl's family, there were his maternal grandparents and two aunts and an uncle from his father's side.

Abraham's mother seems to have been the one who tended to the running of the house. His father, a merchant, was until the very end of his life the respected leader of the local B'nai B'rith lodge and the small Jewish community in the Hanseatic town. Despite his strictly orthodox background, Karl's father was neither intolerant nor lacking in common sense. When Karl wrote, for example, that by taking up the post of psychiatrist at the Dalldorf Hospital in Berlin he would not be able to observe Jewish dietary laws or Shabbat, the Sabbath, his father replied that on a matter of such import to his future the decision had to lie solely with him. By the time Abraham left the paternal home to pursue his higher education, he had, in fact, already abandoned every religious observance and become a lay thinker.

Between Karl and his father there had always been mutual respect and affection.[3]

Whereas his elder brother had been nudged towards following in his father's footsteps (one of the reasons why his brother's unhappiness was felt particularly acutely, according to Hilda, Karl's daughter and author of his biography), Karl had been luckier and allowed to follow his own bent.

As the second-born son, Karl did not find himself up against his mother's overprotection. Although a positive woman, his mother seems to have passed her excess worry on to her first-born, who suffered from asthma attacks, and she restricted her sons during their childhood and adolescence from doing any kind of sport. It was not until his university days that Karl had the chance to engage in sport, mountaineering becoming his great passion.

Abraham was a particularly bright and able pupil. His flair for languages came through during his adolescent years when he developed a keen interest in comparative linguistics. His daughter, Hilda (Abraham, H., 1974), wrote of an exercise book written by the fifteen-year-old Abraham which contains "Abipon Grammar", the language of the Abipones, a South American Indian people, a "List of Indo-Germanic roots", "the word 'father' in 320 languages including Asian, African and Australian languages", "Notes on the Mexican Language", a brief piece of work on agglutination, that is, combining root words to form compound words, and some general notes on etymology.[4]

It is hardly surprising that Karl wished to study comparative linguistics with a professional career in mind. He was not, however, granted financial support by his family to pursue such an uncertain future, and, during a family meeting, was invited to study dentistry instead.

In 1885, he began a course in dentistry at the University of Würzburg, but at the end of the first term he informed his family that he would rather study medicine. After his first examination at the faculty of medicine, Abraham moved to the University of Freiburg, where he remained until the end of his studies, his doctoral thesis being on an embryology-related topic.

The first post Abraham took up was at the Berlin Municipal Asylum in Dalldorf (renamed the Wittenau at a later date). There, under Dr Liepmann, a neuropathologist of some renown, he expected to carry out research in neurohistopathology. This experience turned out to be somewhat disappointing though, there being little debate or fostering of ideas to break the weary routine.[5]

While at the Dalldorf, Abraham had, however, come into contact with patients who had been hospitalised for severe mental, manic–depressive, or schizophrenic disorders (the last of these known then by Kraepelin's term, dementia praecox), and during this period he wrote several neuropathological papers on apraxia and progressive palsy.

This was also when Karl met the woman he was to marry in 1906 and with whom he would have a lasting relationship until the end of his life. Hedwig was her name. She came from a very united Jewish family, had a predilection for English, and an exceptionally acute sense of humour.

In Zurich

Since no other psychiatric hospital in Germany appealed to Abraham, he decided to apply for a post of doctor's assistant at the Burghölzli psychiatric clinic in Zurich. Under the direction of the enlightened Professor Bleuler, this clinic was rapidly becoming one of the world's most important psychiatric university hospitals, surpassing even the prestigious Munich university clinic where the eminent psychiatrist, Kraepelin, had taught.

On the basis of observations and a wealth of statistical data, Kraepelin had encoded a diagnostic distinction between manic–depressive insanity, paranoia, and a third condition he called "dementia praecox". Syndromes such as catatonia, hebephrenia, and paraphrenia, considered separately until then, all came under dementia praecox. Kraepelin's new conception rationally organised the mottled and ill-understood world of psychiatric disorders. His intuition was that each of the three basic groups—manic–depression, paranoia, and dementia praecox—had not only distinct psychological symptoms, but also, as a rule, a precise course and end result. What characterised dementia praecox, for example, was that if the illness did not recede shortly after onset, the patient's condition would relentlessly deteriorate.

Bleuler, however, at Burghölzli, intuited that the illness could be stopped and its course even reversed in some cases if a personal relationship was established with the patient. Together with the prescription of tasks to keep the patient in touch with reality, this relationship could prevent regression and bring about major improvements.

Under Bleuler, Burghölzli was literally turned into a large experimental laboratory and a hub of innovative ideas on patient care. By recruiting young, motivated doctors who underwent what could be described as an intensive psychological approach to severe mental illness, Bleuler also successfully accomplished the unprecedented feat of ensuring that the patient was provided with a satisfactory medical staff. Thus, the Burghölzli university hospital, under Bleuler, became a model for the treatment of mental illness.

The patient was placed at the centre of care and visited twice a day by the doctor, who noted down everything, comprehensible or not, that the patient said. Three times a week the medical staff would come together to discuss each separate case and be constantly updated on new developments in specialist literature (Kerr, 1993). It was Bleuler's wish to apply new techniques developed from psychology laboratory experiments (such as Jung's "associative experiments", innovatively applied by him to schizophrenia) in order to better understand the patient. He was one of the first in the academic world not only to have kept an open mind and been attentive towards psychoanalytic intu- itions that Freud was promoting, but also to have actually put them into practice.

With the open-minded but judicious Bleuler and the spirited and passionate Jung at its helm, nowhere was more willing and able than the Burghölzli clinic to accommodate nascent psychoanalytic thought. This was the dynamic scientific context that Abraham entered at the end of 1904, and where he developed a keen interest in his work, having found a climate that was more favourable to his professional development.

Jung welcomed Abraham warmly: together they took part in "Freudian Society of Physicians" meetings held in the hospital itself, at which psychoanalytic texts were discussed in an effort to then apply them to clinical cases. This friendship was not long-lived, though. By the winter of 1906–1907, relations had already turned cold, to the point that their respective spouses made no further contact with one another.

When Abraham began writing to Freud in June 1907, he ignored the fact that Freud and Jung were weighing him up. In communicat- ing his favourable impressions to Jung, Freud asked what Jung's were. In his letter of 19th August 1907, this was his reply:

> There are no objections to A. Only, he isn't quite my type. For instance, I once suggested that he collaborate on my writings, but he declined. Now he pricks up his ears whenever Bleuler and I talk about what we are investigating, etc. He then comes up with a publication. Of all our assistants he is the one who holds a little aloof from the main work and then suddenly steps into the limelight with a publication, as a loner. He is intelligent but not original, highly adaptable, but totally lacking in psychological empathy, for which reason he is usually very unpopular with the patients. I would ask you to subtract a personal touch of venom from this judgement. Apart from these cavilings, A. is an agreeable associate, very industrious and much concerned with all the bureaucratic affairs of the clinic, which nobody can say of me. (McGuire, 1974, p. 32)

Freud agreed with Jung on some points only and commented, almost as if seeking to allude to something in Jung that would have become increasingly problematic, "I was predisposed in Abraham's favour by the fact that he attacks the sexual problem head on" (McGuire, 1974, p. 34).

Abraham's reasons for keeping his distance from Jung were just as valid. His marked independence forbade him to accept the subordinate role that Jung perhaps required of him. Then, if we give credence to Jones, it seems that Abraham was perturbed by Jung's inclination towards astrology and mysticism. Abraham's character was very different from that of his Swiss colleague and their conflicts were essentially a blend of dissimilar personal characteristics and truly divergent scientific views.

What seems to have won Freud over was this new pupil's scientific method and approach, which came through in his first scientific productions. Endeavouring to systematically extend the research field of nascent analytic theory, Abraham adhered completely to psychosexual theory and the concept of the libido, formulated a short time beforehand by Freud in *Three Essays on the Theory of Sexuality* (1905d). He was not in the slightest close to Jung's spiritual concern, it not easily lending itself to being circumscribed by theory.

Jung, on the other hand, had distanced himself almost at once from Freud's concept of the libido. In "Symbols of transformation" (1911), he used this idea merely as a means to examine myths and symbolism of the Jewish, Christian, Greek, Oriental, and primitive cultures, for instance. Understandably, from his own point of view, Jung could categorically state that Abraham was intelligent but not original.

It was at the First Psychoanalytic Congress in Salzburg in 1908 that the rift between the two opened up. Despite the small number of participants at this first international encounter, not more than around forty, it was a particularly important event, none the less. Freud spoke on the "Rat Man" for approximately five consecutive hours, and both Abraham and Jung gave a talk on dementia praecox.

Abraham's work took as its starting point Freud's conception of libidinal regression and the hypothesis of an original form of auto-erotic pregenital organisation, which, in dementia praecox, stops affective relationships from working. Jung did consider libidinal theory but, at the same time, advanced the hypothesis of a toxic origin in dementia praecox.

Abraham, during his talk, made no mention of the fundamental writings by Bleuler or those by Jung on dementia, the latter being angered to the point of informing Freud of his disapproval. In response to the reprimands and repeated calls to end the dispute, Abraham in the end acknowledged that he had, in fact, omitted the references, which his written copy contained, not out of a question of space, as he had originally thought, but because he had objections towards Bleuler and Jung. It was mentioned that he had to omit the references on the grounds that Bleuler and Jung had distanced themselves from the theory of psychosexual development.

The clash aside, Abraham had his mind firmly set on developing analytic theory just as Freud had presented it, whereas Jung was already beginning to diverge. Long before Freud, Abraham had sensed that Jung was changing tack. Freud, although concerned, was intent on averting the danger of Jung's possible defection, failing to recognise that Abraham's stance was right and his early understanding of what was in the making exact. Certainly, there was rivalry between Abraham and Jung, but this by no means excluded what the former had clearly picked up on.

In Berlin

Abraham had gone to Switzerland with the intention of staying there for quite some time, but he soon understood that, as a foreigner, achieving recognition and career advancement would be far from easy. With moving back to Berlin in mind, where, on the strength of his psychiatric and psychoanalytic knowledge he wished to work independently, Abraham submitted his resignation and left the hospital in November 1907.

On 6th October 1907, he had written to Freud,

> To be sure, there is no shortage of neurologists in Berlin, but I am building my hopes on two factors: first, the use of psychoanalysis; and, second, my psychiatric training, which all Berlin doctors lack completely. (Falzeder, 2002, p. 8)

And again on 13th October

> In Zurich I could breathe freely again. No clinic in Germany could have offered me even a fraction of what I have found here. That is also why I do not find it easy to leave. (Falzeder, 2002, p. 10)

Freud supported his project and invited Abraham to Vienna, where the two met up on 15th December. Abraham was thirty-one years old at the time, and Freud twenty-one years his senior. The latter was a generous host. He paid for his young pupil's hotel and had two small Egyptian statues left in Abraham's room before his departure for Berlin. This marked the beginning of a fellowship that was to last for the rest of Abraham's life.

During this first encounter, Freud and Abraham talked at length, each getting to know the other, their swift scientific exchange, to which their correspondence bears witness, getting off the ground here. Abraham stayed in Vienna for quite a number of days and, on 18th December, attended one of the well-known Wednesday Society meetings, at which sexual trauma and sex education were discussed. From the minutes of that meeting, Abraham stressed how important it is for parents to provide their children's sex education. Staying on the subject, Freud went on to state how parental prohibition can foster extensive pathological repression in the child.

Writing to Eitingon, who was still studying medicine and with whom Abraham had struck up a close friendship while in Zurich, Abraham stated that conversations with Freud went well into the night. Freud divided his followers into three grades: those belonging to the lowest, who understood no more than the *Psychopathology of Everyday Life* (Freud, 1901b), those belonging to the second, whose understanding went no further than the theories on dreams and neuroses, and those in the third grade, who followed him into the theory of sexuality and the libido concept. Abraham stated that he was glad to be included in the third level and was not terribly enthusiastic about Freud's pupils, whom he found very much lagging behind their master. Federn and Rank made the best impression on Abraham, whereas Stekel seemed superficial and Adler factious.

From that time on, Abraham was a close friend of Freud's and one of the few people who were regularly invited to visit him during the holidays. It actually appears to be the case (as Cremerius stated in the introduction to the Italian edition of the works of Karl Abraham, Cremerius, 1969–1971) that between 1907 and 1924 not one piece of work by either of the two escaped reciprocal debate.

Initially, it was Abraham who approached Freud for his help and opinion. As had been the case with Amenhotep IV (Abraham, 1912), which was twice reworked, Freud would make his suggestions and

Abraham write them down. Over time, though, the relationship between the two changed, and the pupil became an interlocutor in his own right. When, for example, Freud sought Abraham's opinion on *Totem and Taboo* (Freud, 1912–1913), unconvinced about the quality of his paper, he was taken by how original his pupil's contribution was.

In December 1907, back in Berlin, Abraham began to work at his private practice and also collaborated with the neurology clinic of Professor Oppenheim, Abraham's wife's cousin. This collaboration was short-lived, though, as Oppenheim was not an advocate of psychoanalysis. Traces can be found, however, in Abraham's correspondence that quite a number of patients came to his practice via the neurology clinic, many of whom were difficult cases. Patient referral of this type begs no surprise considering Abraham's interest in severe illness, which he went on to study tenaciously.

During this time, Abraham was committed to promoting psychoanalysis, which he did by holding seminars at his home and by taking part in debates at local medical societies. The academic and professional world in Berlin being impervious to the new psychological theories, Abraham resented that his attempts to establish scientific contacts with the scientific community ended in failure.

As Jones wrote, when Abraham presented a paper at the Psychiatric Association on "Intermarriage between relatives and neurosis", Ziehen found Abraham's hypotheses bewildering and uncalled-for, Oppenheim had furious outbursts at such monstrous ideas, and Braatz claimed that "German ideals" were being put at stake, adequate measures needing to be taken to put a stop to it.

Otto Schutz-Hartheck's review of Abraham's work on Giovanni Segantini in an important journal of psychiatry clearly illustrates these standpoints.

> It is pointless to go into the details of this paper. One could not object sufficiently to the endeavour of its author, who is overly disposed to exposing himself to ridicule. For those who seek erotic themes in art, that art ceases to be art. I hope that Freud himself is horrified by this latest product of his school. (Le Rider, 1982, translated for this edition)

Fleiss was the only person who warmly welcomed and collaborated with Abraham during this time: no one else referred such carefully chosen patients suited to psychoanalytic treatment as he did.

Then, in 1909, when Eitingon arrived in Berlin, Abraham found himself at last with a valid collaborator by his side.[6]

March 1910 was when the Berlin Psychoanalytic Society was set up, the International Psychoanalytical Association being created that same year. Only several months later were local societies opened in Zurich and Vienna.

Abraham was to be President of the Berlin Psychoanalytic Society for fifteen years until his death. From Jones, we know that in his institutional role, Abraham was able to stand his ground without resentment, and so had opponents but not enemies. He dedicated much to scientific work and carried out a huge amount of clinical work daily. It was his habit to inform his Berlin colleagues of his papers before they went to print or were presented at congresses. At times, Freud would amicably reproach Abraham for the great effort he put into his therapeutic work at the expense of research and the publication of scientific papers, and advised him to increase his fees in order to make more free time for himself.

How important Abraham was to Freud cannot be underestimated. They had met at a time when psychoanalysis was coming out of isolation and needed strong, clear, organised minds through which it could gain a firm foothold. Abraham was an exceptionally able organiser and scientific collaborator. An unwavering, independent thinker and given to frankness besides, he could adopt, even at pivotal moments, an uncompromising stance towards Freud.

Abraham's relationship with Freud did not stop at their constant exchange of psychoanalytic intuitions, but became increasingly important in affirming Freud's ideas and leadership within the psychoanalytic movement. During disputes that would periodically unsettle the group of followers, Abraham always gave his support to Freud, thus preserving unity and safeguarding the growth of the movement. Such was Abraham's moral rigour and coherence that he could perceive potential crises capable of tearing the group of close collaborators asunder even before Freud himself understood the dynamics, he often appearing blinded by hope and affection.

Within a short space of time, Abraham became Freud's devoted correspondent and confidant, sharing with him his successes and also his bitter disappointments on their common path. Both took up the habit of signing their letters "C. C.!", a playful allusion to an anecdote of Abraham's. During a mountain excursion, the two Italian guides who were accompanying him could stave off their hunger no longer and had to resort to eating meat that had gone off, there being nothing else available. Urging the other on, and resigned to their fate, one said to his compatriot, "Coraggio Casimiro!" ("Go on, Casimiro!") So, when they had a bitter pill to swallow, Freud and Abraham would brace themselves with the motto "Coraggio Casimiro!".

I mentioned earlier the "personality" clash with Jung in Zurich and the subsequent scientific squabble at the Salzburg congress. When the conflict with Freud became irreconcilable, Abraham took it upon himself, in January 1914, to write a review of *The Theory of Psychoanalysis* by Jung. What he wanted to demonstrate was that Jung's line of thought was drifting away from psychoanalytic theory: Jung no longer accepted, for instance, the theory on infant sexuality, the importance of the drives, or the Freudian method of interpreting dreams.

After the break with Jung, Abraham was co-opted on to the Committee (Jones having recommended its creation to Freud) with the task of guiding the psychoanalytic movement and keeping it in check so as to prevent further splits.[7]

Within the committee, Abraham came across as a member who naturally commanded respect and a colleague who was able to debate on matters of importance responsibly and without emotions getting in the way. Of the circular letters exchanged between the members of the "committee of the seven rings", this having been their efficient means of communication on the movement's particularly important issues, the most accurate and carefully written were those sent by Abraham.

Worthy of mention is the tone of pained frankness with which, in 1924, one year before his death, Abraham addressed Freud with regard to Rank, whose position was increasingly jeopardising the unity of the psychoanalytic movement. Freud, appearing irresolute, reproached him.

Abraham replied as follows:

Do you remember that after the first Congress in Salzburg I warned you about Jung? At the time you rejected my fears and assumed that my motive was jealousy. Another Salzburg Congress is just around the corner, and once more I come to you in the same role—a role that I would far rather do without. If, on this occasion, I find you ready to listen to me despite the fact that I have so much to say that is painful, then I shall come to the meeting with a hope of success.' (Falzeder, 2002, p. 486)

The situation in the meanwhile having been settled with Rank, Freud failed to understand Abraham's stance. He therefore pressed him to resile from this position in relation not only to Rank, but Ferenczi, too, the latter also having felt involved in the dispute. Abraham's answer was calm and clear. Upholding his view but, at the same time, acknowledging Freud's regret over the matter, Abraham sought to accompany him while he bore the unbearable, yet another painful loss of a friend and colleague.

As Sachs wrote in 1926 (p. 200),

> If, on the one hand, Abraham showed absolute loyalty towards Freud and the psychoanalytic movement, on the other, he preserved his independence and was never afraid to express his doubts and objections if, in his opinion, there were objective reasons for doing so. (Translated for this edition)

After the Salzburg Congress in 1924, at which Abraham and Jones ably settled the conflict with Ferenczi, while Rank distanced himself definitively from the movement (Anna Freud being elected to take his place on the Committee), Freud congratulated Abraham on being elected President of the International Psychoanalytical Association, and wrote to him,

> As regards the scientific aspect, I am in fact very close to your standpoint, or rather I am growing closer and closer to it, but in the personal aspect I still cannot take your side. Though I am fully convinced of the correctness of your behaviour, I still think you might have done things differently. (Falzeder, 2002, p. 500)

Despite recognising in hindsight his being in the wrong, Freud could not forgo defending himself.

The analyst and organiser

Abraham was the training analyst of colleagues who went on to become influential members of international psychoanalysis: Helene Deutsch, Edward Glover, James Glover, Melanie Klein, Sándor Radó, and Theodor Reik. The last of these, Reik, received a monthly cheque from Freud for two years and was analysed by Abraham free of charge.

Despite being one of the few analysts who, together with Freud, was not analysed, Abraham felt the need to stress the importance of undertaking personal analysis to those wishing to enter the profession. Visibly enduring his role as President of the Local Society, together with being the personal analyst of colleagues residing in the city, Abraham gratefully welcomed Hanns Sachs' arrival in Berlin in 1920, as it was he who then carried forward the task of training analyses.

Abraham played an active role at the Psychoanalytic Polyclinic in Berlin, where the work was demanding and psychoanalytic treatment was provided at a low cost or completely free of charge. Co-founded in 1920 by Abraham, Simmel, and Eitingon, one important purpose of the Polyclinic, the main running of which was borne by Eitingon, was to create a teaching context for, and broaden the application of, psychoanalysis. In a letter to Freud dated 27th June, 1920, Abraham outlined the general conditions for accepting candidates at the polyclinic:

Our conditions for working . . . are:

1.) sufficient previous neurological and psychiatric experience; 2.) sufficient knowledge of psychoanalytic literature; 3.) personal analysis of the candidate, which Sachs will undertake. (Falzeder, 2002, p. 429)

The Berlin group, with Abraham at the helm, was the first to ensure its aspiring analysts high-quality training, which is why it then became the organisational model that other societies based their training on, the Society in Vienna included, and the International Association gradually adopting it, too.

The Berlin Institute attracted colleagues from most corners of Europe: besides the previously mentioned analysts and those in analysis with Abraham, others that went to Berlin were Karen Horney and Ernst Simmel, Alix Strachey from England, and Franz Alexander and Therese Benedek, both from Hungary.

Much is owed to Abraham for his contribution to setting up other psychoanalytical centres, too, the British Society, for example: it was Abraham who analysed Sylvia Payne, Edward Glover, and James Strachey. Several pioneers of psychosis treatment, such as Otto Fenichel, Frieda Fromm Reichmann, and Edith Jacobson were also Abraham's pupils.

Karl Abraham had the firm conviction that in order to give impetus to the psychoanalytic movement and enable it to take root as a scientific discipline, new analysts needed proper professional training. This was a much-debated topic at the Budapest Congress in 1918. Up until that point, in order to become a psychoanalyst it was sufficient, but not indispensable (as Abraham's case illustrates), to undergo a brief personal analysis and bury oneself in psychoanalytic literature. Acquiring technique could be learnt through experience and studying Freud's writings on the subject.

Believing not in spontaneous but structurally organised training, Abraham became a member of the Commission for the Education of Psychoanalysts. This saw him actively take part in selecting, analysing, and preparing seminars for candidates, thereby contributing at both local and international levels.

Abraham was one of the few analysts who presented a paper at every congress. In 1922, at the seventh Congress, he was elected secretary of the International Psychoanalytical Association and, at the eighth, appointed President. He also dedicated himself to editorial work, being on the board of the *Zentralblatt für Psychoanalyse* and the *Internationale Zeitschrift für Psychoanalyse*, and replacing Jung as editor-in-chief of *Jahrbuch der Psychoanalyse*, a post he held for the remainder of its day.

During the First World War, Abraham's military assignment took him to East Prussia as chief physician of psychiatry in the Twentieth Army Corps. There, involved relentlessly in medical work, he wrote some important papers, including one on the war neuroses. While serving in the military, he contracted several illnesses that he got over only gradually, not recovering until 1924.

After these complaints came the onset of his lung condition, which led to his premature death. He had accepted the medical diagnosis of bronchiectasis infected by a foreign body, remaining optimistic and not doubting for a moment that he would recover. He had, in fact, presided the ninth Congress in Bad-Homburg from 3rd to 5th September, the first at which he did not, however, present a paper. Under enormous strain, as well as under the influence of morphine to calm his cough, he looked poorly. Then, in the autumn, while in Fleiss's care, he seemed to have regained his health.

During these last months of his life, he had an umpteenth clash with Freud. A scriptwriter, Hans Neumann, and a film director,

George Wilhelm Pabst, sought Abraham's scientific expertise for a film that would illustrate the fundamental mechanisms of psychoanalytic treatment through an episode of a man's life. The title was *Secrets of a Soul*. Abraham saw it as an opportunity to promote psychoanalysis. Therefore, he wrote to Freud that he was tending towards accepting, as doing otherwise could leave the way open for "wild" analysts practising in Berlin to seize this opportunity for themselves. Freud was perplexed, but left Abraham the liberty of coming to his own decision.

In the meantime, several colleagues from Vienna had taken similar initiatives that interfered with Abraham's and had urged him to unite with them. Others publicly dissented, though, and Abraham, set on going ahead with the project, was once more accused by Freud of being unyielding.

This was Abraham's reply:

> In almost 20 years we have had no differences of opinion, except where personalities were concerned whom I, very much to my regret, had to criticize. The same sequence of events repeated itself each time; you indulgently overlooked everything that could be challenged in the behaviour of the persons concerned, while all the blame—which you subsequently recognized as unjustified—was directed against me. In Jung's case your criticism was that of "jealousy"; in the case of Rank "unfriendly behaviour" and this time "harshness". Could this sequence of events not be the same once again? (Falzeder, 2002, p. 564)

Freud's answer was just as clear-cut and sincere:

> Dear Friend,
>
> I note with pleasure that your illness has not changed you in any way. . . . It does not make a deep impression on me that I cannot be converted to your point of view in the affair B-St film. There are things that I see differently and things that I know differently. . . . You were certainly right about Jung, and not quite so right about Rank. . . . It does not have to be the case that you are always right. But should you turn out to be right this time too, nothing would prevent me from once again admitting it. (Falzeder, 2002, p. 566)

Freud, in fact, did not really seem to lend much importance to the film, which, viewed today almost one hundred years on, despite seeming a little naïve and didactic, is not without appeal.[8]

His concern instead lay with the health of his friend, who seemed to be denying just how serious the situation was. Upon Freud's request, Felix Deutsch travelled several times from Vienna to Berlin to visit Abraham and get an exact sense of things. Around the middle of December all hopes were shattered. Sachs sent Jones a telegram: "Abraham's condition hopeless" (Jones, 1953–1957, *Volume 3*).

Karl Abraham passed away on Christmas Day, 1925, at the age of forty-eight.

Freud sent his wife a heartfelt letter:

> Since my telegram on receiving the news of your husband's death I have put off writing to you. It was too difficult, and I hoped it would become easier. Then I became ill myself, became feverish, and have not yet recovered. But already I see that putting it off was pointless, it is just as difficult now as it was then. I have no substitute for him and no consolatory words for you that would tell you anything new. That we have to submit with resignation to the blows of fate you know already; and you will have guessed that to me his loss is particularly painful because I think, with the selfishness of old age, that the loss could have easily been spared for the probable short duration of my own life. (Falzeder, 2002, p. 568)

Memorial services were held in Vienna, Berlin, New York, and Moscow the following January and February. Freud attended the ceremony in Vienna, breaking his habit of absence from the Vienna meetings for this one occasion. The death of Abraham aroused intense emotion among psychoanalysts. Volume 2, issue XII of *Internationale Zeitschrift für Psychoanalyse* was dedicated entirely to Abraham's memory.

Eitingon, Abraham's right-hand man, was appointed President of the International Psychoanalytical Association, while his pupil, Ernst Simmel, who played an important role in running the Berlin Psychoanalytic Institute, was elected President of the Berlin Psychoanalytic Society.

CHAPTER TWO

A summary of Abraham's most important works

braham did not leave particularly voluminous psychoanalytic papers. His more than 120 articles, spare and concise, span all areas open to psychoanalysis at that time, but are not particularly extensive.

That emotion and powerful inspiration that come through in Freud's prose is not found in many of Abraham's works. Keeping to an impersonal, almost doctor-like style, his writing tends not to enthuse. Perhaps this is why, despite being appreciated within the psychoanalytic community, Abraham has not had much appeal to a wider public. Originality and attentive clinical observations always feature in his papers, but some of his work, his earlier writings especially, are in-depth accounts of points found in Freud's theories.

The most frequent topics he wrote on were the interpretation of dreams, the libido, infantile sexuality, biographical essays, studies on folktales and myths, various clinical topics (hysteria, alcoholism, perversion), and problems concerning analytic technique. His works on dream symbolism indicate the home or garden as the maternal symbol, the serpent as the dangerous paternal penis, the spider as an invasive mother, and obscurity as the maternal womb: these symbols, for Abraham, represent meanings that are universal and univocal.

His writings on psychosis, melancholy, and technique is where we especially find his original thinking. And no less important are his biographical essays and those on character.

Early writings on psychosis and trauma

The high opinion of Abraham that Freud expressed to Jung in 1907 was in reference to Abraham's first two psychoanalytic essays: "On the significance of sexual trauma in childhood for the symptomatology of dementia praecox" (Abraham, 1907a), a paper presented at the annual meeting of the Berlin Psychiatric Society, and "The experiencing of sexual trauma as a form of sexual activity" (Abraham, 1907b). In these two short papers, Abraham advanced some thoughts on the importance of trauma and the relevance of infantile sexuality to the onset of illness in adulthood. These ideas were based on observations of clinical cases from which aetiological hypotheses were then drawn.

In the first essay, Abraham asked himself why there was a high incidence of infantile sexual trauma among psychiatric patients. His view is that some children, driven precociously towards sexuality, provoke the encounter with the adult, unaware they are doing so, while others are passively subjected to sexual trauma. In these cases, the children feel guilty about the event and conceal it. Sexual pleasure arouses strong feelings of guilt in the child, this being the main reason why the trauma is repressed and, in turn, exists outside consciousness.

Sexual traumas suffered in childhood can return to the psychotic adult, providing a theme for delusions and hallucinations. Only in some patients can sexual trauma be traced back as a co-factor of the illness. In others, the traumatic event is testament solely to early access to sexuality.

Abraham did not see trauma as the aetiological factor in illness, but a determining factor in the kind of symptoms that would develop.

In his second paper, "The experiencing of sexual trauma as a form of sexual activity" (1907b), Abraham faithfully referred to Freud's thought on infantile sexual trauma, which was no longer considered a pathological agent in neurosis. Hypersensitivity and an over-reaction to sexual stimuli are cited as determining factors, it often being the case that children with a tendency towards sexual excitement can occasionally become involved in sexual relationships with the adult.

If trauma is severe, what is it that makes some children suffer while others manage not to? As in his first piece of work, Abraham noted that some children are complaisant towards the person making sexual advances, whereas others suffer the seduction and keep quiet about it. The trauma is experienced internally as a form of sexual activity, and, as such, it is a source of shame and so undergoes repression. If a child has shown no sign of unconscious compliance, the traumatic experience is more likely to be communicated to an adult. This child who reacts is less likely to fall ill than the child who is complaisant, who, while ill, is likely to have similar experiences repeatedly.

Abraham connected this susceptibility to trauma with an unconscious masochistic wish that often manifests in individuals who, as children, were deprived and distressed. The predisposition to neurosis or psychosis lies in the tendency to repeat the sexual trauma.[9]

Brought out by Abraham in these two writings is the "traumatic" dimension and how it contributes to determining both the symptoms and course of the illness.

Barale and Ucelli (2001) underline that

Through his in-depth account of two cases of female patients suffering from dementia praecox, in the "secondary" psychotic production, of which traces of traumatic sexual experiences suffered in childhood clearly come to the fore, Abraham convincingly shows how a series of experiences that are overburdened, have never been mentally metabolised and have never really belonged to the subject's "history", in that they have never been integrated or experienced but are "foreign bodies", or a threat to self-sentiment, can burst in via the hallucination and delusion along routes that are very similar to those described by Freud in the dream or in hysteria. (Barale & Ucelli, 2001, p. 697, translated for this edition)

To illustrate how Abraham's conception of sexual trauma was never simplistic, the two authors added,

The psychopathological structure is not "explained" at all in terms of its historical precedents, which can by no means be reduced to an objectively "traumatic" dimension. Abraham hypothesised what we may refer to as a "circular" relationship among the elements. (Barale & Ucelli, 2001, p. 697, translated for this edition)

They continued,

> In psychosis and events that are what Abraham referred to as intolerable to the sentiment of the self, mental life fails to constantly seek to reorganise the traumatic base, which it feeds on, into a horizon of meaning. In this empty space, void of meaning and utterability, the trauma "returns", so to speak, from the outside as a hallucinatory or delusional re-elaboration. Psychotic productions may also be seen as seeking to do this, not due to their being "produced" by the trauma, but because the traumatic element is expressed through them. (Barale & Ucelli, 2001, p. 698, translated for this edition)

Another important part of Abraham's early scientific output is "The psychosexual differences between hysteria and dementia praecox", presented at the Salzburg Congress in 1908 (Abraham, 1908). This essay was a first attempt to apply psychosexual theory to psychotic disorders, connecting the illness in adulthood to vicissitudes of early child development.

With this work in mind, Freud wrote that

> As early as 1908, K. Abraham asserted, after a discussion with me, that the principal characteristic of dementia praecox (which may be considered one of the psychoses) is *that there is no libidinous occupation of objects*. But then the question arose, what happens to the libido of the demented, which is diverted from its objects? Abraham did not hesitate to give the answer, "It is turned back upon the ego, and *this reflected turning back is the source of the megalomania* in dementia praecox". (Freud, 1920, p. 358)

From his observation of hospital patients, listless and isolated, Abraham noticed that they manifest a complete break with their surrounding reality. Unlike neurotic patients, who are conflictual and contradictory in their relationships, dementia praecox patients are so completely unable to transfer their libido on to external objects that they are locked in their affective experiences.

He went on to say that neither the hysteric nor the schizophrenic child is able to establish a normal relationship with his parents during childhood, but whereas children with hysteria are excessively attached to one of their two parents, dementia praecox patients structure indifference or hostility towards them. At times, this indifference and hate can, however, be preceded by an initial period of excessive attachment. These patients do not exercise the normal process of repression that leads to modesty, compassion, or disgust, and so, consequently, their behaviour is characterised by exhibitionist, eroticised, or regressive-faecal tendencies. According to Abraham, these different ways derive from an overflow of libido that fails to be properly channelled. This results in repression and sublimation being defective, which, in turn, prevents the normal stages of development in early infancy from being reached.

Furthermore, dementia praecox coincides with a massive regression to infantile autoerotism. Whereas the delusion of grandeur can be traced to an afflux of libido on to the ego, the persecutory delusion, on the other hand, originates out of the patient's terror of an empty and threatening external world. Hallucinations are the result of repressed wishes that encounter a fragmented ego. The "dementia" does not concern intellectual performance, which remains potentially intact, but emotions. These become distorted or completely numbed.

Several years after Abraham had written this paper, Bleuler (1911), in his famous monograph on schizophrenia, introduced the concept of autism, which bore similarities to Abraham's description of autoerotism.

This paper by Abraham, which takes its place alongside the finest intuitions on psychosis, is the earliest attempt to formulate a psychoanalytic theory on psychosis and it has served as a base for further developments on this subject.

Freud himself wrote that Abraham's paper "contains almost all the essential views put forward in the present study of the case of Schreber" (Freud, 1911c, p. 70). And in his letter of 18th December 1910, Freud wrote to Abraham that in the Schreber case he followed "the path indicated by your paper on the psycho-sexual differences between hysteria and dementia praecox" (Falzeder, 2002, p. 122). That megalomania is the sexual overestimation of the ego is an idea developed by Freud. It is worth noting that the concept of autoerotism is Freud's, too: it appeared in a letter to Fleiss of 9th December 1899. Here, Freud claimed that autoerotism is the deepest layer of sexuality and that the autoerotic drive re-emerges in paranoia (Castiello D'Antonio, 1981).

This is Barale and Ucelli's comment (2001):

Abraham defined autoerotism as a direct expression of the "psycho-sexual" side of the illness, and he described a fluctuation of psycho-sexual stages and positions along a developmental path that was neither linear nor monolithic but exposed to regression and progression, that is, to a multitude of possibilities all occurring simultaneously, to a multitude of psychosexual (and ego-world relationship) patterns that are closely correlated to life's vicissitudes. These elements are kept in dialectic tension with great equilibrium to avoid any kind of short circuit or simplification. (Barale & Ucelli, 2001, p. 702, translated for this edition)

His works on depression

Having decided to leave the psychiatric clinic, Abraham had no choice but to give up his research on dementia praecox and shift his attention towards depression, an easier condition for him to observe, given the type of patients that sought his help.

At the Weimar Congress in 1911, he presented a paper on "The psychosexual basis of agitated and depressive states", which he developed further and published in full in March of the following year entitled "Notes on the psycho-analytical investigation and treatment of manic–depressive insanity and allied conditions" (Abraham, 1911b). The first of three papers that make up Abraham's contribution to the study of depression, here he drew a parallel between anxiety and depression, two manifestations frequently found in melancholy: "Anxiety and depression are related to each other in the same way as fear and grief. We fear a coming evil; we grieve over one that has occurred" (Abraham, 1911b, p. 137).

Abraham believed that ambivalence between hate and love is more deep-rooted in the depressed patient than in the obsessive neurotic patient. The former indiscriminately directs his hate against all individuals, and, by projecting hate outwards, the melancholic patient perceives others as hostile and tends to think they isolate him because of his illness, unaware that the hatred is his own. He admonishes and torments his objects, and himself, his masochism being an expression of gratifying a wish, a megalomaniacal wish that he carries out in his claiming to be the biggest criminal on earth.

In the depressive phase, failing to positively achieve drive gratification brings on a feeling of impoverishment, whereas, during the
manic phase, when drives are not subjected to the ego's control,
the patient is granted a superior sense of strength. Important is Abraham's comment that both phases, despite their apparent differences,
derive from the same affective complexes. Without underestimating
the difficulties, Abraham pointed out that psychoanalytic therapy can
be effective for treating depression.

> It is usually extraordinarily difficult to establish a transference in these
> patients who have turned away from all the world in their depression.
> Psycho-analysis, which has hitherto enabled us to overcome this
> obstacle, seems to me for this reason to be the only rational therapy to
> apply to manic-depressive psychoses. (Abraham, 1927[1911b], p. 153)

Later, when discussing the narcissistic transference, Abraham
examined these difficulties in greater depth.[10]

Still on the subject of depression, "The first pregenital stage of the
libido" was written in 1916 while Abraham was doing his military
service in Allenstein: he sent it to Freud as a gift for his sixtieth birth-
day. In his usual manner, Abraham began by referring to pregenital
libido organisation, pointing out that whereas sado-anal organisation
had been investigated in depth in psychoanalytic literature, the oral
stage had received much less attention.

Based on a previous paper presented to the Berlin Society in 1913,
in which Abraham had sought to examine the relationship between
nutritional and sexual instincts, he once again claimed that what prin-
cipally characterises the oral stage is that the instinct is autoerotic and
rests on the extremely important function of preserving life through
the consumption of food.

He distinguished between (a) cannibalistic oral organisation,
where sexual activity is not yet separate from the consumption of
food, and the sexual aim consists in incorporating the object, and (b)
sadistic-anal organisation, in which active–passive antagonism is
predominant, and the appropriation instinct employs body muscle for
the active aim and erogenous intestinal mucous as a passive sexual
aim.

A series of clinical situations are described in a bid to show how
oral erotism is maintained in numerous habits of adult life. Although
the two functions, erotic and nutritive, may either coexist or remain

distinct, conflicts connected to the oral sphere lead, respectively, to eating, sleeping, and language disorders. When the nutritional function is excessively charged with sensuality, the libido remains anchored to primitive forms of satisfaction, failing to move on towards higher object relational functions.

An excess of oral libido is expressed through the neurotic wish to eat sweet things, or "neurotic hunger" attacks. It is also found in behaviours where the use of stimulants replaces satisfaction obtained via normal libido investment. Vice versa, in some women there is often a connection between libido repression and neurotic hunger.

Abraham observed that oral pleasure fosters the development of fantasising. Also, when auto-erotically invested, the oral zone serves to prevent depressive experiences: the sole fact of having a pill to swallow can improve one's mood. Oral fixation, when a reduction in pleasure looms, leads to the onset of depressive psychic states.

When the mouth is overused as an erotogenic zone, it can no longer carry out functions that are asexual: this type of patient might, for example, be unable to speak or eat. Others will use the mouth perversely. Abraham cited the case of a rather quiet and isolated seventeen-year-old male who would bite his lips, draw his cheeks inwards, suck continuously, and use his tongue to caress or tickle his palate. Through these voluptuous sensations, he reached oral masturbation proper. When he found himself in the company of another man, he would have the obsessive phantasy of putting the man's penis in his mouth. In others' company, he was hardly able to speak or eat: his mouth was unable to perform functions other than sexual.

Another example of excessive oral erotism that Abraham provided was that of a schizophrenic male patient who, despite being given to anal and genital masturbation, maintained a high investment in the oral zone. For a long time this patient showed exclusive interest in his own body, above all, in anal and genital sensations: he would be dedicated continuously to masturbation. Although he used many parts of his body, he took particular interest in his mouth, so that when he mentioned waking up during the night because of an exciting dream, saliva dripping from his mouth, he would speak of "ejaculation from his mouth". In the grip of strong sexual desire, he would drink milk that had to be body temperature and if, by chance, none was to be found, he would calm his excitement by masturbating. The patient's associations continuously went from sucking milk to ingurgitating food. As a child, the idea of loving someone was equivalent to eating something good: he had "cannibalistic representations", wanting to swallow his governess, "skin, hair, clothes, and all" (Abraham, 1927[1916], p. 257). He wished to bite her breast . . . This patient had experienced major difficulties during weaning and it was this that Abraham communicated.

At the root of some oral problems are environmental factors, others having individual factors at their base. Some babies, for instance, readily accept changing over to a bottle, given that milk flows more freely this way; some categorically refuse to detach themselves from the breast, and others have trouble giving up the bottle or some equivalent. In common to all these situations is that the nutritional and sexual instincts have not separated, but remain intertwined.

Conflict between oral erotism and other life investments can lead to difficult compromises. Some people, who can often be efficient and competent in their professional life, can be conditioned by their auto-erotism, which gets in the way of fulfilling tasks. One patient may not be able to concentrate on intellectual work until having masturbated, another might have to have a pen in his mouth, or gnaw at his fingers, and so forth.

In neurotic patients, Abraham stated, oral libido demands constant gratification: autoerotism must be satisfied to prevent the person from falling into depression. Other typical symptoms of a depressive symptomatology are disgust, nausea, vomit, or a lack of appetite. In yet other patients, especially in cases of involutional depression, the fear of starving to death is predominant. And depressive psychotic phantasies often feature the delusional representation of being turned into a ferocious, man-eating animal.

By analysing disorders related to consuming food, refusing to nourish oneself and fearing death by starvation, Abraham was able to further his considerations on the psychogenesis of depressive disorders and acknowledge, via the constellation of symptoms just described, that melancholy belongs to the oral stage of development. The melancholic patient's pain is rooted in his perception of limited vitality and deteriorated genital libido. That the libido regresses to the cannibalistic oral stage reactivates unconscious desires of incorporation: this is why the depressed patient wishes to swallow objects up, thereby annihilating them.

Alongside ambivalence and sadism, which are common to both depression and obsessional neurosis, peculiar to melancholy is the tendency to devour the love object: ". . . in his unconscious the melancholic depressed person directs upon his sexual object the wish to incorporate it. In the depth of his unconscious there is a tendency to devour and demolish his object" (Abraham, 1927[1916], p. 276).

For Abraham, this oral-sadistic object relation is what causes the melancholic's constant self-reproaches, which serve to keep his unbearable wishes of cannibalistic incorporation away from consciousness.

> If we assume that the deepest repressed wishes of the melancholic are of a cannibalistic nature, that his "sins" in their essence refer to a forbidden, even detested, act of eating, then we understand the great frequency with which he refuses to take food. (Abraham, 1927[1916], p. 278)

The nutritional function goes back to being experienced as a cannibalistic act, just as it was at the beginning of life: the patient must eschew food to fight off his sadistic impulses. The unconscious perception of feeling guilty is provided with a path of atonement via conscious reproaches. Even though, objectively speaking, the melancholic is innocent, he "knows" he can consider himself a master criminal. Abraham mentioned the case of a patient who feared being transformed into a wild beast capable of devouring his peers.[11]

"A short study of the development of the libido, viewed in the light of mental disorders" is Abraham's third and final work on manic–depressive psychosis. Written in 1924, it is a continuation of two other papers, the first read at the Berlin Psychoanalytic Society, and the second presented at the International Congress in Berlin in 1922.

For many reasons, the title of the paper does not quite fit its contents. Written several years after Freud's "Mourning and melancholia" (1917e), it provides a conclusive understanding of melancholic states, and smoothly integrates Freud's work. Abraham recapitulated his observations on the relationship between melancholy and obsessional neurosis to stress the point that depression is connected to a more primitive developmental stage. Both illnesses benefit from "free intervals", a concept Abraham repeatedly mentioned to underline the advantages of therapeutic work during periods of remission. From a symptomatological viewpoint, during the free interval, the melancholic patient and the obsessional patient resemble one another. Embracing Freud's intuition that, having lost his object, the melancholic patient is driven to aggressively reintroject it (which is why self-reproaches concern the lost object), Abraham reasserted that this incorporation derives from a regression of the libido to a cannibalistic stage.

By introducing the idea that the various stages of psychosexual development are two-phase, depending on whether sadistic or strictly erotic aspects are predominant, Abraham specifically identified the oral-sadistic stage as the starting point of depressive development. The pathology of the obsessional patient, on the other hand, in it being anchored to the second stage, sees a sadistic use of products of excretion.

The melancholic patient moves between the oral-sadistic pole of cannibalistic incorporation and the anal-sadistic pole, where the object is expelled and annihilated like faeces. The phantasy of eating excrement, that is, of reintrojecting a dead object and expelling it, is sustained by this dual polarity, and it constitutes punishment for guilt related to having unconsciously killed the love object.

The most interesting section of the paper is "Object-loss and introjection in normal mourning and in abnormal states of mind", where Abraham stated that the psychology of mourning is not adequately understood. What is actually meant by normal mourning? Why does it take place and what processes are involved in detaching from the lost love object? Paradoxically, the dynamics of melancholy, in which self-reproaches to hit out at the love object prevent the love–hate conflict from being solved, are perhaps clearer.

In "Mourning and melancholia", Freud stated that memories and expectations connected to the lost object are re-evoked one by one and the libido is slowly withdrawn from each of these. Abraham made an important addition that went one step further: he claimed that in *normal mourning* the real loss of the object is followed by the *introjection of the loved person*. This reintrojection is what enables normal mourning to be overcome.

He identified the mourning process at work in a patient's dream. This patient dreamt that he was attending the autopsy of his recently deceased wife. The scene of the autopsy resembled slaughtered animals on display in a butcher's shop. At a certain point, the various parts of the corpse were joined back together and the patient's dead wife began to show signs of life. For Abraham, this dream announced the success of "the work of mourning": the love object is no longer lost since the patient puts it back together again, to be carried inside him, alive, never to be lost again. In normal mourning, the lost object is reanimated so that it can be set up in the ego.

Whereas Freud underlined a gradual easing of suffering due to the pressures of reality, Abraham stressed the importance of introjecting and re-establishing the lost object as an internal object. He hypothesised that, in healthy individuals, mourning occurs via archaic mechanisms in our lower psychic strata: it is here that the analogy with the process of melancholy lies. The essential difference is that in melancholy "taking the object inside" occurs via a conflict of ambivalence and identification with the object. The depressed individual is unable to separate from the object and remains joined to it through a bond of suffering he tortures with, and is tortured by. Reanimation underlying the work of mourning cannot, therefore, take place. The lengthy nature of working through mourning is not because of the adhesiveness of the libido to the lost object, as Freud had suggested: the internal object, experienced as torn asunder and destroyed, needs to be put together again and reanimated.[12]

In a clinical case of a homosexual patient's mourning, Abraham described an equally important stage of working through, which is idealising the object as a defence against depression. Even though the patient's mother was dead, for a long time he had the feeling that he always carried her with him and was supported by the splendour of the beloved and lost object. Reversing Freud's description that "the shadow of the object fell upon the ego" meant that Abraham could describe how the idealisation of the love object serves to deny the loss by means of illusion.

In the section "Notes on the psychogenesis of melancholia" (1924), Abraham once again differentiated melancholy from dementia praecox: whereas, in the latter, withdrawal occurs within indifference, in depression, the loss brings suffering and unhappiness. This loss, however, is apparent only as, in melancholy, there is overinvestment in the ego. Analytic investigation has unveiled that the melancholic patient cultivates inside a sense of superiority: during sessions, for instance, he does not listen to the analyst's comments, or does so with an air of condescension, and is convinced that the therapy is nothing other than shallow.

The "delusion of inferiority" that psychiatry described consists, in fact, in an unconscious grandiose delusion. The depressed patient overestimates the effect his thoughts, affects, and actions have: thinking, for example, that he is the biggest criminal on earth, he believes in the grandeur of his own hate. Oscillation between love and hate, between overestimating and underestimating himself, is an aspect of the patient's narcissism (positive or negative).

Whether one becomes melancholic as opposed to hysterical or obsessive seems to depend on a combination of factors working together. The first is constitutional and corresponds with a strong original oral-erotic charge. In depressive states, there is a particular kind of nostalgia for everything that is related to the maternal breast and parental caring, almost as if it were testament to an addiction that was never overcome. Individuals so characterised are extremely demanding and react strongly to frustration. As a psychic factor here, Abraham indicated early injuries to infantile narcissism by the mother after an initial privileged period. Disappointment and frustration at the peak of maternal attachment, which coincides with oral sadism, result in the introjection of the object charged with hate. Abraham pointed to repetition of the primary disappointment in later affective relationships as an important element for the onset of depression. Each new sentimental relationship connects back to the trauma and to the reactive hate of the first "disappointment in love":

> The disappointment which the melancholiac has suffered as a child at the hands of his mother while he was still in a markedly ambivalent state of feeling has affected him in such a permanent way and made him so hostile to her that even his hatred and jealousy of his father has become of minor importance. (Abraham, 1927[1924], p. 460)

Afterwards, Abraham toned this down, stating that ambivalence regarded both parents, even though "*in melancholia the whole psychological process centres in the main around the mother*" (Abraham, 1927[1924], p. 461, my italics).

Further on, he added that in order to fully understand the melancholic's hostility towards his mother one has to remember that the primal castration, the original castration, is the withdrawal of the breast. The unbearable disappointment inflicted by the love object makes the melancholic disparage it and equate it with body content that may be expelled and annihilated. As a form of narcissistic identification, from here the object is introjected and devoured. Abraham described the *infantile prototype of melancholic depression*, which coincides with a form of original dejection. This complex situation with the mother does not help the child when he has to deal with the Oedipus conflict. The rejection the child is up against combines with the exciting phantasies of what occurs in his parents' bedroom. Unable to reconcile love with irreducible hate, he falls prey to a feeling of despair, which is the state of mind that most resembles melancholy.

Mania, on the other hand, according to Abraham, is an easing of the unrelenting critical control of the ego ideal on the ego. The "shadow of the object which had fallen on the ego" fails, allowing narcissism to produce a positive, pleasant mental state. No longer disturbed by the superego, the libido is once more directed towards the world of objects; the patient gobbles up his food and swallows whatever comes his way. Incorporating objects is followed by expulsion that is just as swift, contact being fast and superficial. If a physiological maniacal reaction follows mourning, the mania constitutes a cannibalistic orgy.

A maniac patient of Abraham's identified with the emperor Nero who killed his mother and planned to burn down Rome, the mother symbol. The maniacal triumph is not a totem feast to attack the father, but a destructive attack against the mother.

In Part Two of the same paper, "Origins and growth of object-love" (1924), Abraham outlined the following model of object-relation development: following the primitive phase of total cannibalism there is another that corresponds to the partial incorporation of the object. It is true that the object is once again robbed, but of a part of its body only; it is maimed but not annihilated.

One female patient had the phantasy to bite off the penis of any man she met and to copulate with a penis without there being a man. The relation and subsequent identification are with a partial object. This patient not only represented men by the penis but represented women by the breast, that *"had obviously been identified in the child's mind with the supposed penis of the female . . . [or] by her buttocks, which in their turn stood for her breasts"* (Abraham, 1927[1924], p. 486, my italics). Partial incorporation is a form of appropriation found in primitive love.

From this viewpoint, fetishism, where excessive value is attached to one single part of the human body, is regression to this stage of relating with the partial object.

Abraham concluded,

Complete and unrestricted cannibalism is only possible on the basis of unrestricted narcissism. On such a level all that the individual considers is his own desire for pleasure. He pays no attention whatever to the interests of his object, and destroys that object without the least hesitation. On the level of partial cannibalism we can still detect the signs of its descent from total cannibalism, yet nevertheless the distinction between the two is sharply marked. On that later level the individual shows the first signs of having some care for his object. We may also regard such a care, incomplete as it is, as the first beginnings of object-love in a stricter sense, since it implies that the individual has begun to conquer his narcissism. But we must add that on this level of development the individual is far from recognizing the existence of another individual as such and from "loving" him in his entirety, whether in a physical or a mental way. His desire is still directed towards removing a part of the body of his object and incorporating it. This, on the other hand, implies that he has resigned the purely narcissistic aim of practising complete cannibalism. (Abraham, 1927[1924], p. 488)

The distinction between a partial and a complete object saw the introduction of new terminology and a new way of understanding infantile relational development. The cannibalistic relation with the partial object represents progress, given that part of the object is spared.[13] Implied is that progress from the primitive to the more advanced relationship is achieved through respect and care for the object and a coming to terms with cannibalistic voraciousness.

Abraham ended the paper underlining the correlation between psychosexual phases of development and their corresponding levels of object relation: the highest is the genital stage, where the individual is capable of loving, and the lowest the oral sucking stage. He described fixation in the different neurotic syndromes relative to the stages of development: first melancholy, then obsessional neurosis, and last hysteria, which he saw as the most advanced stage. He also drew up a general character table to facilitate envisaging together all object-love developmental stages and various forms of neurotic suffering. Since there is initially an absence of objects, a "pre-ambiva-lent" stage exists, which is conflict free.

> We regard the earliest, auto-erotic stage of the individual as being still exempt from instinctual inhibitions, in accordance with the absence of any real object relations. In the stage of narcissism with a cannibalis-tic sexual aim the first evidence of an instinctual inhibition appears in the shape of morbid anxiety. The process of overcoming the cannibal-istic impulses is intimately associated with a sense of guilt which comes into the foreground as a typical inhibitory phenomenon belong-ing to the third stage. The third stage, whose sexual aim is the incor-porating of a part of the object, is left behind when feelings of pity and disgust arise in the individual and cut off this form of libidinal activ-ity. In the next stage, that of object-love with the exclusion of the genitals, inhibition takes the form of feelings of shame. Finally, in the stage of real object-love we find social feelings of a superior kind regu-lating the instinctual life of the individual. (Abraham, 1927[1924], p. 496)

Abraham underlined that ambivalence towards partial objects (penis, breast, excrement) gradually changes to a feeling of contempt, towards excrement in particular, which becomes the object of refer-ence: ". . . he identifies the person whom he rejects with disgust with faeces" (Abraham, 1927[1924], p. 497).

Besides Abraham's attempt to hierarchise the object relation, I find his intuition on anxiety as a precursor to a sense of guilt particularly interesting.[14]

The essay ends drawing a parallel between embryogenetic pro-cesses and psychosexual development. The erotogenic function of the anal zone in ontogenetic development is advanced as follows: at an early stage, the intestinal canal is connected to the neural canal, or canalis neurentericus (stimuli thus pass from here directly to the nervous system), and the anus is nothing other than a primitive mouth that has migrated down to the posterior end.

In this last piece of work on melancholy, Abraham was finally able to formulate a complete and accurate theory on depression. He defin-itively identified the sadistic polarity of the oral and anal stages as the fixation point of the illness. He also went back once more to the idea that the mother is the child's object of hate. On the one hand, the depressed patient seeks to incorporate his mother, but, on the other, he makes her the object of sadistic attacks: he desires her castration or her death.

It is in this paper that the concept of the "bad mother" (May, 2001) begins to take shape. Although the term was not used at the time, Abraham employed "wicked" three times to stress that hatred towards the mother differentiates melancholy from the other neuroses. I mentioned earlier how Abraham sought to tone down the fact that anger is towards the mother, claiming that it is directed against both parents, which was clearly in order not to distance himself too much from Freud, who placed in the foreground the conflict with the father. At any rate, Abraham later confirmed that the mother is central to the melancholic's psychological problem.

He was to underline this once again in the second edition of the biographical study on Segantini, written and published in 1925, not long after "A short study of the development of the libido, viewed in the light of mental disorders". He stated in this biography that the mother is always the cause of frustration and disappointment, which is why she becomes the object of the desire for revenge.

Contributions to therapy and psychoanalytic technique

Abraham's intuitions on the psychology of dementia praecox and melancholy form the core of his literary output on psychoanalytic theory, but also numerous are his works in the area of analytic clinical practice. I shall look here at a paper written on analytic technique in 1919, "A particular form of neurotic resistance against the psychoanalytic method", that anticipated subjects which were only clearly developed several decades later.

Here, Abraham described the analytic course of those patients who observe the fundamental rule of free association in appearance only, producing, in actuality, a continuous verbal flow which is its antithesis, that is, programmed as opposed to "free". In these cases, resistance to analysis is concealed behind this seeming willingness to co-operate: the patients are engaged in continuous discourse with the analyst, by whom they feel easily humiliated and from whom they fear interpretations, because of their own personal sensitivity.

When they bring a dream to the session, it is spoken about or described in detail, but not beyond its manifest content. Surrounding themselves in a cloud of words means these patients are in an environment of gratifying pleasure, somewhere pleasant and protected. This "resistance" can also take the form of phantasies about their own analysis: idealising their neurosis, they believe they are of particular interest to the analyst. Some patients expect their biography to make a contribution to psychoanalysis or think they can be superior to those peers towards whom they harbour feelings of inferiority.

As opposed to seeking a dependence relationship, these patients, driven by their envy, wish to substitute the analyst. Abraham observed that this type of patient prefers to talk about psychoanalysis rather than let the analysis take its course. The premeditated nature of their associations is a sign of their intention to steer the analysis: the analytic material is, therefore, laden with a heavy narcissistic stamp. Given that interpretations are not accepted, the analysis can easily turn into a verbal dispute about "who is right". Patients of this kind are very demanding and constantly expect to be at the centre of the analyst's attention, distancing themselves when they have the slightest impression that they are not. This is why their positive transference is unstable and flighty.

Abraham stressed here the role of *envy*: it derives from the patient's perception of the analyst's good qualities, it works against analytic progress and it activates defences of self-sufficiency and omnipotence. Auto-analysis, or, rather, work the patient thinks he is doing on his own when he is not with the analyst, is considered superior to that done in the session. It is not, however, reflective or creative, but a form of masturbation, a sort of daydream. And since change is sacrificed for the sake of narcissism, these patients' analyses become particularly long and arduous.

For Abraham, it was of the utmost importance to analyse the narcissistic transference right from the beginning and interpret the patient's defiance as a sort of revolt against dependency on the father; only by overcoming the narcissistic constraint in favour of a positive transference can progress be stepped up.[15]

In a short but interesting work on analytic technique, written also in 1919, "The applicability of psycho-analytic treatment to patients at an advanced age" (1919b), the reader marvels at its highly accurate clinical observations and clear presentation of concepts that went against some predominant beliefs among Abraham's colleagues, all backed up with examples from clinical practice. Here, he wrote of better articulating Freud's judgement, which was probably misunderstood or uncritically applied, on the effectiveness of treatment diminishing the more advanced the patient's age. It was Abraham's view that analysis, an empirical science *par excellence*, should not stop at *a priori* assumptions but verify whether and under what conditions it can achieve results. Despite the then widely held belief among analysts that it was increasingly difficult to obtain positive and long-lasting results the greater the age of the patient, a belief Abraham, too, had shared initially, his experience with older analysands led him to change his mind. After examining the results, it became clear that the more successful cases were those in which patients had developed severe neurotic symptoms at a mature age. Only for those patients in which the neurosis had manifested fully in early or late childhood, or even in adolescence, were the results less promising. *"We may say that the age of the neurosis is more important than the age of the patient"* (Abraham, 1927[1919b], p. 316, my italics).

Therefore, similarly to dementia praecox, the neuroses, too, are more difficult to treat when onset is during childhood or adolescence and symptoms persist over time. Yet another observation Abraham made is that a patient's relatively mature age does not prevent early childhood conflicts from being relived via the analytic process.

The paper ends with an invitation to investigate and better understand why some young patients are refractory to psychoanalysis.

Studies on character formation

Abraham's principal work on this subject is "Psycho-analytical studies on character-formation" (1921–1925), composed of three essays:

1. "Contributions to the theory of the anal character" (1921);
2. "The influence of oral erotism on character-formation" (1924);
3. "Character-formation on the genital level of the libido" (1925).

Drawing on works by Freud, Sadger, Ferenczi, and Jones and connecting clinical observations to the study of character, Abraham described two separate anal character types that may even be present simultaneously in the same individual. The first is characterised by excessive courtesy, the second by rebelliousness. For different reasons, these patients end up creating difficulties in analytic work: the former tend to let the analyst do the associative work, and the latter enter into a defiant and diffident relationship with the analyst.

Abraham believed that situations that reoccur in the analytic relationship and evoke transference resistances have their beginnings during the child's education in sphincter control, and arise from early injury to infantile narcissism, from parental pressure to submit and from the child's rebellious responses.

He also pointed out that envy, a devastating emotion, goes back not to anal, but oral, sadism.

In the second essay, on the oral character, Abraham maintained that every event that is related to psychosexual development brings with it a mixture of primitive and advanced developmental forms. He believed that in every later phase of development, traits remain from earlier phases: each erotogenic zone preserves the dynamic characteristics of the one that preceded it. When illness of an anal character presents itself, the anal phase is built upon the rubble of oral erotism, it already being anomalous by this stage. Whatever the case might be, introjection, possession, and restitution, the dynamic elements of the more developed relation carry with them the original and persistent oral experience.

Whereas pessimism and severity of the anal character coincide with a highly frustrated and dissatisfied oral experience, a good oral experience in infancy is what an optimistic character rests on. Should frustration occur in the second period of the oral stage, when biting connected to teething brings pleasure, hostile impulses and ambivalence towards the mother will be stronger.

On the "genital" stage of development, the third essay examines the problem of so-called normality. Abraham stated that psychoanalytic thought does not easily lend itself to establishing a difference between what is "normal" and that which is not. What he stressed is that the individual's development (and, therefore, the concept of normality) rests on the progressive transition from primitive to more advanced forms of organisation. Since not one stage of development is completely overcome or disappears without leaving a trace, it is difficult to establish how and to what degree primitive organisations persist into adult life without excessively compromising the stable acquisition of adult characters.

Whereas early character forms are under the sway of narcissistic impulses, the "normal" character should coincide with a relatively un-narcissistic personality. Also marking maturity is a progressive move away from original ambivalence, which manifests as excessive oscillation between one affective extreme and its opposite.

In addition, Abraham pointed to the importance of care, which, when lacking, can have catastrophic effects on the child's character.

Other works by Abraham explore difficulties and distortions in the relationship between the two sexes. The first, "Ejaculatio praecox" (1917), examines the complex and difficult relationship men have with women; the second, "Manifestations of the female castration complex" (1920), identifies female animosity towards men.

In the first, we find a description of the premature ejaculator's phallic–urethral narcissism; as opposed to desiring sexual intercourse, he would rather urinate on the female. Narcissistic phantasies in which incontinence implies the idea of greater performance prevent acknowledgement of the disorder. Also, the image of the patient's parents' intercourse as a sadistic act derives from a violent attack against, and Oedipus conflict with, a devalued father. In the analysis of these patients, what emerges is an object relation of hate towards a despised and devalued mother. An infantile conflict that was not worked through affects the oedipal area, resulting in a relationship full of vengeful contempt towards the female figure.

In the second piece of work, "Manifestations of the female castration complex", Abraham re-examined the Freudian theory of gender psychosexual differences. What he highlighted, however, is the difficulty the female has to go through in order to accept a passive position. Returning to the subject of penis envy, he explained further why, in these cases, women overestimate the male figure. Devaluation of the female figure, in his opinion, is where strong envy towards the male has its beginnings. In some cases, female unhappiness can derive from displacing penis envy from the father to the mother because of the children she possesses.

An interesting observation Abraham made is the potential effect the mother has on her children: by depreciating men, she devalues female sexuality and negatively influences the female identity of her daughter; with relational problems such as these, that is, demeaning the male mind and body, the mother wounds her son's positive narcissism. Abraham underlined that it is the mother and not the father who decisively influences the children: it is maternal envy that distorts the child's sexual development, not castration anxiety.

Psychoanalytic biographies

Worthy of mention are Abraham's two works dedicated to the psychological study of famous individuals, Segantini and Amenhotep IV. They are essentially attempts to understand in depth their character and creative gift through the lens of their early affective life.[16]

Although among Abraham's first, both writings reflect great psychological depth and an engaging narrative structure. Central are the arguments that infantile vicissitudes explain the individual's crises in adulthood, and that one of the roots of creativity is infantile conflict that has not been worked through.

In the first analytic biography, "Giovanni Segantini: a psychoanalytical study" (1911a), Abraham outlined the artist's personality and the unconscious sources of his creativity. He connected the unconscious death wish to Segantini's trauma in childhood, thus advancing what he believed lay at the root of his melancholic disposition. Orphaned at the early age of five and moved back and forth between relatives and reformatories, Segantini's childhood was a troubled one. Yet, as Abraham said, he was a great artist, animated by a flurry of thoughts and a wealth of noble feelings. Where, then, did his creativity come from?

This was Segantini's answer, ". . . to obtain a satisfactory explanation one would probably have to descend to the very depths, and in that way study and analyse every emotion of the soul right down to the first" (in Abraham, 1927[1911a], p. 214).

Underpinning Segantini's creativity was his love for his dead mother, who became an ideal figure in his mind. This interiorised object that his thoughts centred on and were sustained by was closely linked to his artistic creativity.

> I carry my mother in my memory, and were it possible for her to appear at this very moment before my eyes, I would still easily recognise her after thirty-one years. I see her in my mind's eye, her tall form walking wearily. . . . When she died she was not yet twenty-nine years old. (in Abraham, 1927]1911a], p. 214)

Despite his loss occurring when he was of a tender age, Segantini showed no sign of complaint or desperation. Infantile ambivalence, which fuels hate and death wishes, was compensated by his ability to sublimate. Some of his better paintings, for instance, centre on portraying enraptured motherhood, a particularly famous one depicting a young, delicate-looking woman holding a chubby child on her lap. And often in his paintings, the beauty of flowers transfigures into female radiance.

However, fear that his birth had harmed his mother's health weighed heavily on Segantini's soul. Abraham suggested that Segantini's creativity originated from his need to recreate life and rebuild something he feared had gone to pieces. Feeling guilty over having possibly caused his mother's death, ever since childhood he was particularly sensitive to loss, pain, and death. Mother, Mother Nature, and the Motherland, in his intellectual and emotional world, were one and the same. He approached these with a particular form of melancholy and compassionate kind-heartedness. Segantini's "sweet melancholy" was a rich source of inspiration to him. Amid the bright, unspoilt nature of the high Alps, the artist's creative impulse was at its best: colours and light were intoxicating to him, the seasons overwhelming.

Later, the pain of melancholy and sorrow returned, to inspire his mystical–phantasy pieces and paintings of his late period; where sympathy and love had been, a sense of distress and death flowed in. *The Punishment of Luxury*, depicting mothers floating restlessly, unprotected, sees vengeful resentment condemning the mother to wander aimlessly for all eternity. Segantini, Abraham wrote, projected outwardly on to the penitent mother all the anxiety and melancholy that he personally suffered at the time he was abandoned. His introversion and solitariness came through more and more in his visionary and phantastical paintings. Escape from reality and attraction to obliteration seemed to be among his final passions:

"Yes, real life is an unending dream, a dream of gradually attaining an ideal, which is so remote and so lofty as to approach the infinite" (in Abraham, 1927[1911a], p. 245).

Traces of cruel suffering tinged by severe trauma, together with visions of exasperated serenity, prevailed in his *"longing to reconcile the warring instincts within him, and to unify life and death into one harmony"* (Abraham, 1927[1911a], p. 250, my italics).

Bearing witness to this longing is his last work, *Triptych: Nature–Life–Death*: the last is what triumphed. Having decided to paint alone up in the high mountains, Segantini became ill, refused medical help, and received care only as he was dying, his palette in hand. Abraham asked himself whether Segantini wanted to go up there, to the high mountain, to live and work, or also to die. Death, never to have left him, was born when he was, despite his efforts to deny, contain, and transform it.

Abraham associated two of Segantini's dreams on death: one, dreamt many years earlier, was imbued with anxiety, and the other conveyed the artist watching his painting, on death, leave his mountain home in a coffin while his wife wept. Before going up the mountain, Segantini reported this one to his wife. Abraham saw anxiety arising from the artist's desire to live in the first; in the second prevail Segantini's submission to, and fascination with, approaching death.

> . . . but the sinister forces in his unconscious ranged themselves on the side of the disease, furthering the work of the destruction and bringing about his death. . . .We know, however, that the man who aspired to encompass with his infinite love every living thing, hid within himself the will to destroy his own life.
>
> Psycho-analytical observation, which gives us an insight into the struggle between conscious and unconscious forces, enables us to understand and to sympathise with this inner duality. It reveals to us the whole tragedy in the life of one who died so young, and who whilst working tirelessly walked ever in the shadow of death. (Abraham, 1927[1911a], pp. 257–258)

In a second edition of Segantini, written in Sils Maria thirteen years later, Abraham wrote of the trauma and mortal blow that a child is unable to recover from when it concerns the irreversible loss of the person that all one's love has been placed in. The loss need not coincide with death, as it had done in Segantini's case, but it marks the destruction of all trust in the world. A child is not equipped in the slightest to deal with such an experience: it is always the mother who causes this disappointment during that first part of infancy.

And, on account of repetition compulsion, the tragedy comes around cyclically throughout one's life. Depression, which brings with it the experience of total abandonment, coincides with the wish to die.

"Amenhotep IV: a psycho-analytical contribution towards the understanding of his personality and of the monotheistic cult of Aton" (1912) is a psychoanalytical reconstruction of the life of this famous pharaoh, who was the founder of ethical and religious reform without precedent. At the early age of ten, he ascended the throne and reigned until his death at twenty-eight. He was intensely attached to his beautiful mother, who came from the East. Married when still a child to his child bride, his bond to his mother accounted for his faithfulness, even when his young wife could not give him a son.

Love for his mother was evident also from the transformation of traditional religion into one single "cult" of the god Aton. Abraham interpreted this feat as a non-violent rebellion against the father. Amenhotep did, in fact, reject his affiliation by replacing the gods and his father with a divine being of a higher nature. He radically affirmed the existence of one spiritual god, thereby turning the traditional structure of Egyptian society upside-down. Unlike his predecessors, who reigned to consolidate political power, Amenhotep instead veered towards sweeping spiritual change, national interest being almost totally forgotten. His God, Abraham pointed out, was even more progressive than the God of the Old Testament. Unlike the warlike God of the Bible who destroys the enemy, he was incorporeal, unbound by human passions, and full of goodness. Songs and hymns dedicated to Aton rang out with praises of love: the ethics of Ikhnaton, the name later adopted by the pharaoh, condemned all expressions of hatred and violence, forbade human sacrifice, and abolished war as an instrument of oppression. Freeing himself from the symbols of power, Ikhnaton was at liberty to live among the people of his land, enjoying family relations and inspiring a new form of simple but beautiful art.

A forerunner of modern and civil morals, the young pharaoh went too far for the times and ignored the laws of politics. Averse to the use of force, he did not act in response to outside attacks, paid no attention to internal uprisings, and did not rush to his subjects' rescue when they called for help. So devoted was he to religion that even in the face of tragedy he proceeded with religious reforms and the elimination of polytheist writings. His ideals, according to Abraham, were so advanced that they were unachievable and might even have been mere daydreams. Ikhnaton's premature death is likely to have spared him from the fate of falling victim to a court revolt. His work and his religion, after his death, were both swiftly destroyed.

Abraham believed that extreme idealisation of the self and the love object (a beloved divine father) was connected to extreme anxiety about violence. Infantile sadism was feared to the extent that aggressiveness could never be expressed, not even in self-defence. And despite Amenhotep's attempt to demolish paternal authority, he coated the new god with the same omnipotence that every child attributes to his father, with whom he wishes to identify.

In many ways, the Egyptian pharaoh was a dreamer who wanted to live in a world of beauty, love, and ideals while keeping at bay pain, grief, and world conflicts. Abraham suggested an analogy between Amenhotep and Phaeton, who was so intoxicated by the shining sun that he soared high, only to then lose control of his horses and be thrown from the carriage to his death. Likewise, on his spiritual journey, Amenhotep dared to fly with his mind to greater heights, only to lose control of the reins of command when blinded by the sun, his land disintegrating in his wake.[17]

CHAPTER THREE

The Freud–Abraham correspondence

Of irreplaceable scientific value is the exchange of letters between Freud and Abraham. In their voluminous correspondence, we are able to gather the beginnings of important psychoanalytic intuitions as well as the contributions each author made to solving some knotty problems on analytic theory and clinical practice. Consistent in pace and of great human depth, this collection of letters appeals to the reader as would a novel rich in humour, which neither protagonist falls short of, especially when it comes to the obtuseness and narcissism of colleagues or rivals.

The dialogue between Freud and Abraham touches on scientific subject matter, research topics, editorial projects, the presentation and discussion of clinical cases, human affairs, family matters, illness, war, and world events. The tone used between the two is free of rhetoric, as becomes a dialogue between friends: without beating about the bush, they can naturally go straight to the point.

Their first letters open with "Dear Professor" from Abraham to Freud and "Dear Colleague" from Freud to Abraham, and then "Dear Friend"; the pupil, however, when writing to his teacher, always maintained his respectful and affectionate form of address.

An example of authentic analytic dialogue, their correspondence contains creative thought, love, and reciprocal respect, and takes the reader through the pair's joint development of valuable analytic intuitions: first comes a question from Abraham who is keen to understand, next Freud's enlightening and balanced reply that always leaves the way open for his interlocutor's response, then the pupil's quick insight and further, more exact observations that lead to yet other formulations.

The topics of greatest importance are most certainly to do with the hard battle to promote psychoanalytic thought, the successes, the setbacks, and the major conflicts concerning Jung, then Rank. No important work escapes exchange between the two, the verdict anxiously awaited as the date of publication draws near. Doubts and perplexities are forwarded when each writes something new, their respective considerations giving us a glimpse into the complex drafting of texts which then went on to become classics.

The principal work-related subjects in common to Freud and Abraham are the psychology of dementia praecox, the discovery of autoerotic investment, psychosis, and last, Abraham's most important area of research, melancholy.

When Abraham read "Mourning and melancholia", which is truly a joint effort, caught quite off guard, he was unable to fully understand several fundamental passages of Freud's text. He thought long and hard before coming up with a solution to the unresolved problem of how mourning is overcome. It is my belief that his solution paved the way for psychoanalytic thinking to establish the theoretical orientation developed by Melanie Klein that went on to be called "object relations". Oddly enough, in a letter written in October 1923, just several months before the publication of Abraham's third work on melancholy, in the correspondence appears the name Frau Dr Klein. Abraham reported to Freud that Melanie Klein was successfully bringing to a close the analysis of a three-year-old boy who faithfully manifested primary depression, *Ur-Melancholie*, and that this case cast unexpected light on infantile instinctual life. What logical and forward psychoanalytic thinking for a man who, just two years later, was to perish.

CHAPTER FOUR

Abraham's scientific contribution

W hen it comes to evaluating Abraham's literary output, the short space of time he had to develop his scientific creativity cannot be overlooked, his analytic studies spanning a mere seventeen years from 1907 to 1924. Although he attentively followed the path his Viennese professor had marked out, ever since he had known Freud his own original and independent thought never failed to come through. Thanks to his keen clinical observation, right from the start he examined with utmost thoroughness those areas of great importance to Freud.

In his first two papers, "On the significance of sexual trauma in childhood for the symptomatology of dementia praecox" (1907a) and "The experiencing of sexual trauma as a form of sexual activity" (1907b), although in agreement with Freud on the importance of infantile sexuality and on there being a constitutional factor in the predisposition to disease, Abraham added that, in some children, there is an inclination to derive pleasure from pain. If, as shown by the clinical data, sexual abuse is extremely frequent among neurotic and psychotic patients (regardless of whether the illness is caused by the trauma), it seems natural to enquire as to why this is so.

Without challenging Freud's view that it is not easy to tell real trauma from traumatic phantasy, Abraham stressed that individuals destined to become future patients are disposed to sexual acting. Intuiting in this way repetition compulsion, that is, actively seeking a traumatic event, Abraham anticipated a concept that Freud was to develop only much later, and he also identified in sadomasochism a first but important correlate of trauma (Good, 1995).

Although an innovator and precursor of psychoanalytic thought, Abraham did not, however, manage to systematically turn his intuitions into one explicit and complete theory.

As Glover stated,

> If we compare his character studies with his essay on libido development it becomes clear that he was not content with mere demonstration of individual stages and presentation of clinical findings, but that his ambition was the correlation of a multiplicity of observations and their co-ordination in a general scheme of development . . . but one has the impression that at the time of his death he had almost brought to completion that particular side of his activities and was about to convert his summation of experiences into new and fruitful generalizations. (Glover, 1928, p. 122)

Therefore, despite his short life, the channels he opened up to furthering psychoanalytic theory and clinical practice deserve to be granted the credit they are due. Several of Abraham's more valid ideas, which merge with the development of Kleinian thought, run the risk of not being fully acknowledged as his.

What instead is unanimously recognised as belonging to Abraham are his extraordinary organisational skills, which he applied widely within the psychoanalytic movement. Many young colleagues, themselves going on to become important psychoanalysts, wanted Abraham as their training analyst, attracted by the sheer force of his structured and coherent thinking. And Glover (1928), for instance, saw in Abraham's clear mind a need to create order out of chaos.

Abraham was a systematic researcher. His starting point never failed to be clinical work from which theoretical generalisations could then be drawn. No topic of research was left to intuition or free creativity: he would systematically retrace his steps, define each one, and integrate it into his ever-broadening perspectives. If Abraham's conception of childhood development is set against Ferenczi's more intuitive and modernist relational approach, what Abraham might lose in one direction he can clearly regain in others, especially if we consider his in-depth understanding of the transference and the narcissistic state.

Deep is his understanding of unconscious hate, too. In the introductory memoir to Abraham in the *International Journal of Psychoanalysis*, Jones (1926) wrote that Abraham's main contribution to psychoanalysis was his deep understanding of problems inherent to pregenital stages of development and the vicissitudes of hate. It is the latter, in particular, which comes up continually in his writings, that paved the important way for a more thorough understanding of the negative transference.

It cannot be said that Abraham was ahead of Freud. He was more of an ideal climbing partner who journeyed by his professor's side, standing out for his quest for clarity and his solid conceptual connections, and not seeming to need, as other pupils did, to differentiate himself too much from Freud. In fact, between the two, there had never been an open scientific conflict. He was not attracted, as was Ferenczi, for example, to routes that at times were ingeniously alternative, and so he ran no risk of scientific isolation or painful backtracking.

Besides the above-mentioned areas, Abraham put his energy into reasserting what this new science had achieved, thereby averting any risk of it being misunderstood. Similarly to Ferenczi and Jones, Abraham entered unchartered waters and worked to consolidate and defend what was still in the making. It seems, however, that many then contemporary analysts could acquire but few elements of psychoanalytic insights due to the fledgling method of passing on technique and theory, not to mention the harshness of the times.

I often find, however, dissimilarly to some, such as Jones, who magnified the quality of his style and writing, that a number of Abraham's texts are excessively weighed down by an impersonal, scientific style. His writing does not always enthuse the reader, who must make a particular effort in order to appreciate the content. That writer who lets himself go, carried by his enthusiasm about a new discovery, is felt much more in the correspondence with Freud than in his scientific papers.

Abraham did, none the less, show tremendous foresight in pinpointing theoretical issues that would go on to be most important for psychoanalytic thought. Glover (1928) pointed out that it was the publication of Abraham's work on libidinal development in 1924 that helped scale down the attraction exerted by Rank's *The Trauma of Birth* (1929), an apparently revolutionary hypothesis that, in essence, was reductionist, despite Ferenczi enthusiastically welcoming it. By presenting a picture of mental health as a complex interweave of internal factors, traumatic impacts, and primitive moments of development, Abraham helped put right the "deviationist" but, above all, simplistic and naïve tendency found in Rank's writing.

Addressed, too, by Abraham was the complexity of analytic clinical work, hence his expository style of writing, which saw the introduction of an analytic report that included the presentation of a case, a discussion on the material, a theoretical summary, and a conclusion. In his mind, only through clinical and therapeutic work could deeper psychoanalytic understanding come about.

Furthermore, by connecting severe pathologies to fixation points in the earliest stages of development, Abraham paved the way for Melanie Klein's work on early anxiety. Still fundamental today is his distinction between autoerotic withdrawal in schizophrenic psychosis and the process of melancholy: in the former, the representation is destroyed, whereas in the latter the representation of the object is introjected and, therefore, remains, albeit marked by sadism.

Important developments in psychoanalysis, still relevant today, are also a result of several of Abraham's intuitions. In a paper presented in 2000 at the Herbert Rosenfeld Conference in London, Ronald Britton outlined the developmental course of the psychoanalytic concept of narcissism, drawing attention to the fact that it was Abraham who highlighted the role of destructiveness and hostility towards the object.[18] Whereas Freud described narcissistic love as replacing or continuing on from maternal love (1914c), Abraham sensed that at the root of narcissism was envy, narcissism being a defence against the development of object love. Britton pointed out that ever since Abraham had met Freud, the former advanced his own original ideas in this area of investigation.

It was as early as 1908 when Abraham underlined, in his paper on psychosexual differences between hysteria and schizophrenia (dementia praecox), that in the latter, the capacity for object love is destroyed. His idea is that an individual in this state of mind withdraws from all libidinal investment and turns towards his own body, in which he erotically invests. It is this insight that led to schizophrenia being psychoanalytically understood as an autoerotic illness (narcissistic neurosis).[19]

The patient's narcissism comes up, too, in Abraham's essay "Ejaculatio praecox" (1917), where he connected it to resistance to the analytic relationship: that the patient himself is the true narcissistic love object means that the relationship with an object cannot be.

Abraham also cast light on a particular form of resistance some patients have to the psychoanalytic method ("A particular form of neurotic resistance against the psycho-analytic method", 1919a) due to the fact that they are unable to form a dependency bond that brings benefit to growth and development. These patients' obligingness is not to be mistaken for co-operation, it being a pseudo bond in order to seductively take possession of the other's good qualities. And, in his 1924 paper on melancholy (it, too, a narcissistic pathology), we can find Abraham's acute insight on self-admiration and self-disparagement, two sides of the same coin. All of these intuitions were taken up by other important analysts and went on to become cornerstones of clinical theory and analytic technique. As cases in point, I should like to mention the concept of the negative therapeutic reaction put forward by Riviere (1936) and Horney (1936), as well as Rosenfeld's (1971) theorising on destructive narcissism, and Steiner's (1987) pathological organisation.

Important, too, is Abraham's contribution to developing therapy for severe patients. Unlike Freud, who no longer took severe patients into his care during the second half of his life, Abraham was more than in a position to write on these cases, as they were part and parcel of his daily analytic work. With this kind of patient, he suggested keeping in mind a developmental path that goes from the most primitive phases to the more developed levels of object relations.

Real recovery, in his opinion, was impossible to predict (given that he did not bring to a close many of his cases, and neither did he have sufficient catamneses), but he could confidently say that change lastingly influences symptoms and behaviour. Even when improvement is only partial, he viewed analysis as being able to remove the patient from his narcissistic withdrawal and bring about greater wellbeing than would spontaneously occur. Moreover, when in analysis, in reaction to a mental trauma, patients disposed to psychotic episodes tend to manifest neurotic symptoms.

"That a psychoneurosis should have ascended from a melancholic to a hysterical level seems to me a significant and noteworthy achievement" (Abraham, 1927[1924], p. 478).

Therapy helps patients to feel supported and build a psychological base that enables them to cope with what would otherwise be unbearable anxiety.

Through his daily work with psychotic patients, Abraham developed a very clear idea of the precise approach this kind of patient can benefit from. As Fenichel pointed out (1945), on Abraham's recommendation the therapist should actively establish and maintain a positive transference, and, above all, he should represent reality and work on the patient's each and every attempt to flee it. All contact with the patient must be put to use, right down to discussing the smallest details of his everyday life. And the transference should not be disturbed too early on through being interpreted, which instead can or must be done in the analysis of neurotic patients. Implicit difficulties aside, Abraham believed that the same setting for neurotic patients needs to be used with psychotic patients, as the difference, in his opinion, lies not in the setting, but in focusing attention on certain aspects of the relation and the transference. His invitation to work during free intervals is a valuable piece of advice in order to establish a deep analytic relationship that can then withstand subsequent psychotic crises.[20]

Analytically studying early infancy and laying down a child therapy[21] are yet other important contributions that Abraham made. Belonging to his group of collaborators were two pioneers of child analysis, Hermine von Hug-Hellmuth and Melanie Klein. Commenting on a paper presented by Melanie Klein at the first German Congress for Psychoanalysis in 1924, Abraham said that the future of psychoanalysis lay in child analysis.[22] He was convinced that the more severe the illness, the more likely it was that there had been a setback that had affected the child during his early development.

Abraham sought to place the various mental disorders on a scale whereby the primitive correlates to the pathological according to the equation primitiveness–severity. Not surprisingly, Abraham never spoke of Oedipus with particular enthusiasm, events from the pre-oedipal stages capturing his attention much more, and about which he had more to say. As opposed to being imbued with paternal rivalry,

Abraham's Oedipus bears the child's pure, passionate love for his mother.

Back in 1909 he had written to Freud,

> Incidentally, are you also of the opinion that the *father* is so predominant? In some of my analyses it is definitely the mother; in others one cannot decide whether it is the f. (ather) or the m. (other) who is of greater importance. It seems to me to depend very much on the individual circumstances. (Falzeder, 2002, p. 87)

From the correspondence, Freud did not provide an answer to his question bar a reference to individual differences.

There had always been, as May (2001) noted, a conflict below the surface between the two over the role of the mother: the child's affective experience with the mother was what Abraham underlined, whereas Freud, even by virtue of his authoritativeness, placed emphasis on the pre-eminence of the father. When referring to Abraham's manuscript on the pharaoh Amenhotep (1912), Freud wrote that it was not clear to him why such great importance had been given to the relationship with the mother, while the conflict with the father had been brought out just slightly. Freud's approval came only once Abraham had evened out his perspective.

The gap between Freud and Abraham regarding the importance of the conflict with the mother and the secondary role played by the father was, in fact, substantial. Abraham, for instance, attributed to the mother the origin of the affective trauma out of which the object relation of melancholy develops. By underlining, as did Freud, the child's infantile tenderness for the mother, the conflict cannot then arise from rivalry with the father.

At the time, the new theory was that hate and desire for revenge are directed not against the parent of the opposite sex but that of the same sex because of rivalry. Abraham, however, dissimilarly to Freud, thought that the child's affective ambivalence was directed selectively against the mother, the first object of attachment love and hate. Painfully rejected by his mother, Segantini's response was one of hatred and death wishes against her: overriding was the trauma of abandonment. This does not cancel out the father's importance, as hate towards both parents plays an important role in giving rise to illness. But love and hate that underlie depression are, in the first instance, determined by the mother.

In Abraham's vision, in comparison to suffering arising from the relationship with the mother, that connected to the role of the father and the Oedipus conflict assumes a modest role. Aversion is not towards a hated rival, the father, and the mother is not solely loved and idealised. It is she, the mother, who is "bad", the child distancing himself from her because of a very specific affective experience: her lack of response to infantile passion. Abraham believed in an original event that was really quite different from that outlined by Freud, who maintained not only that Oedipus and the conflict with the father were decisive, but that they were also universal. Anxiety at the threat of castration was not what Abraham identified as the trauma, but the love object's betrayal of the child at a tender age in which the mind is unable to tolerate the injury, let alone understand why it comes about. The violent, destructive reaction this provokes arises from the vengeful nature of infantile love. It was Freud himself, was it not, who rightly said, in "Instincts and their vicissitudes" (1915c), that first comes hate, which is more powerful than love. The concept of destructive hate, in reaction to the trauma, is an extremely important point in Abraham's analytic theory. The illness develops out of the combined effect of the trauma and a specific psychosexual organisation. The destructive response is that of an infant not yet able to tolerate pain and whose only option is to mobilise revenge and sadism. Abraham's insight here, originally advanced in his essay on Segantini, was later drawn upon many times over. At a theoretical level in his writings on melancholy, he expressed this same concept as the cannibalistic incorporation of the love object under the sway of oral sadism.

In their theorisation of melancholy, it could be said (May, 2001) that Freud placed emphasis on depression, narcissistic identification, non-differentiation between the ego and the object, alteration of the ego, and conflict within the ego; Abraham's focus, on the other hand, was firmly on the role played by infantile sadism. I see this as one of the reasons why Abraham initially missed taking in the revolutionary perspective put forward by Freud on depression in "Mourning and melancholia" (see Appendix). For Abraham, the incorporation of the object in melancholy, which occurs under the sway of a destructive desire, is key, whereas the core issue raised by Freud of identification and the narcissistic relationship between the ego and the object left him quite indifferent. The destructive desire is not original, according to Abraham, but always results from an affective trauma.

Unlike Klein, who underestimated the importance of trauma and neglected its impact, hinging her theory on the instinctive nature of sadism and the infant's earliest destructive phantasies, Abraham insisted that hate is unleashed because of the loss of the love object. But let us read what Klein had to say in the introduction to *Envy and Gratitude* (1957) about her scientific connection to Abraham and an extremely important point of his theory.

> Abraham explored the roots of destructive impulses and applied this understanding to the aetiology of mental disturbances more specifically than had ever been done before. It appears to me that although he had not made use of Freud's concept of the life and death instincts, his clinical work, particularly the analysis of the first manic-depressive patients to be analysed, was based on insight which was taking him in that direction. I would assume that Abraham's early death prevented his realizing the full implications of his own findings and their essential connection with Freud's discovery of the two instincts. (Klein, 1975[1957], p. 177)

I am not so sure that Abraham would have fully endorsed his former pupil's words. Moreover, *Beyond the Pleasure Principle* was written in 1920, five years before Abraham's death. It was here that Freud introduced the dualism of the life and death instincts and the importance of the destructive impulse, but I am unaware of Abraham ever having mentioned this work by Freud, perhaps because the concept of the death instinct itself and the vision of both instincts (life and death) neither impressed him nor stirred his enthusiasm.

Although Abraham stressed the importance of destructiveness but, at the same time, differentiated himself from Freud, who was pressing ahead with the pleasure principle, he did think that hate and sadism seep into the libidinal relationship, without ever constituting a separate and contrasting instinct, though. Hate, in his mind, is always mixed with love.

Even when Abraham considered envy, he did so by understanding it as an oral character trait that is, in turn, connected to the sadistic–anal impulse. The death wish he spoke of, therefore, has absolutely nothing to do with the death instinct in the Freudian or Kleinian sense. In the biography of Segantini, Abraham described, with deep emotion, the experience of the artist's early loss of his beloved mother, a loss which inflicted intractable pain. Segantini's unconscious sadism was an exacerbated reaction to a trauma that was impossible to work through.

Abraham, who was the first to investigate oral and anal sadism, had no need whatsoever to believe in the dualism of the instincts, which would even have eclipsed the importance of the trauma. Acknowledging the primitive nature of the impulse, that is, the destructive cannibalistic character with which it incorporates, is sufficient to explain the annihilation of the love object.

As opposed to suggesting a primitively destructive child, Abraham involves us in the child's dreadful difficulties when he is left with no choice but to tackle conflicts that are too big for him to cope with. Unable to reconcile love and hate, the small child falls prey to a feeling of dejection, which is the prototype of subsequent depressive crises. Abraham did not present a unilateral vision of the child, or place particular emphasis on the trauma, or on an adult world that lacks comprehension for the child, as Ferenczi was later to do; neither did he portray the child as a poor creature left to fend for himself in the face of overbearing adults. He gave importance to the child's character disposition and underlined the importance of the terrain the trauma operates on as well as the need to love in order to overcome hate.

Not without reason was it Abraham who discovered the relationship between normal mourning and melancholy. Hatred towards the object that disappointed is a cornerstone of Abraham's vision of mental suffering. Facing loss, the drive disposition towards hatred is a decisive factor in order to give shape to mourning, or, *vice versa*, to melancholy. The primary object's responsibilities and the tendency the child's character has to becoming a prisoner, trapped, can trigger a vicious circle.

Abraham's analytic legacy mainly consists in his fundamental insight into ways in which mourning may be overcome. These are the ideas that were followed up and extended to then come together in Klein's works "A contribution to the psychogenesis of manic–depressive states" (1935) and "Mourning and its relation to manic–depressive states" (1940).

As for processes of mental growth, Abraham's intuition on the oral, cannibalistic, and possessive character of the love relation opened the way to furthering understanding here. As Lebovici (1978) wrote, incorporation is a phantasy, introjection a process. Incorporation, as

Abraham was the first to explain, is taking the object inside via a body–mouth phantasy, to then eat it and greedily draw its good qualities. Introjection (or interiorisation) goes hand in hand with the constitution of the affective world and looks to the object as though it were a whole. Incorporation takes inside only that which is desirable, rejecting or vomiting up what is unknown or bad. Introjection discriminates and accepts.

The incorporation–introjection–identification transition is the normal developmental process. Abraham's insight led to fundamental progress in understanding normal processes of mental development as well as mechanisms that are at work in the course of analytic treatment.[23]

The importance Abraham gave to mechanisms of introjection and projection, his insight into the role sadism plays in early infant development, the weight he lent to destructive and cannibalistic phantasies, his work on mourning and melancholy, the stress he placed on the mother and the loss of the breast, his description of the narcissistic transference and character, and his shifting the libidinal and aggressive conflict from the penis to the breast, remain, to this day, the foundation stones of the psychoanalytic edifice.

The Kleinian model of the therapeutic relationship and analytic process was built on these intuitions. If mourning and separation are fundamental to firmly establishing a good object in one's inner world, it then follows that analytic therapy needs to provide a course of treatment bearing close analogies with the transition from melancholy to the mourning process. Ambivalence and hate must be remedied through the new therapeutic experience, which needs to modify the relationship with the original object and facilitate integrating past and present experience.

Abraham also outlined the transition from incorporation (under the sway of cannibalistic orality) to introjection (interiorisation). Thus, he built a psychopathological model that sees a traumatic factor and a constitutional impulse converge. I see this model as having opened the way for the relational, or object relational, conceptualisation that Klein later developed. The traumatic factor is early maternal betrayal (abandonment) that encounters primitive sadistic impulses that are peculiar to the precise moment the trauma occurs. The relationship with the object, henceforth marked by resentment, brings on mental suffering that will subsequently lead to depression.

Immensely inspired by Abraham's work and appreciated to the present day is the Kleinian model, which sees the primitiveness of oral sadism producing phantasies of attacking and devouring the object. In the face of primary destructiveness (which then came to correspond to envy), a sense of guilt and a desire for reparation are later mobilised. Here, the therapeutic process entails gaining awareness of the love–hate conflict through the mobilisation of attempts at reparation.

With the introduction of splitting and projection (projective identification) to Kleinian theory, the analyst's focus is on reintegrating the projected parts of the patient's personality during his therapy. The receiver of the patient's projections and split-off parts is the analyst himself, who, according to Freudian technique, is the mirror image of the patient's past. The here and now is of greater importance within this approach than is reconstructing the past. Through systematically analysing the transference, the analyst tries to help the patient retrieve an image of his internal world in which libidinal as opposed to destructive aspects prevail. The former emerge only when split-off parts, unconscious due to the very fact they contain envy, are experienced as one's own, after which reparation can then be set in motion. Starting from his study of the analytic relationship and the negative transference, it was Karl Abraham who rendered this path of development feasible to analytic theory and clinical practice.

One hundred years on from Abraham's birth, Lebovici (1978) reminded us of this when he wrote,

> From this point of view, Karl Abraham was a pioneer, but he remains a model for today's psychoanalyst. He uses detailed descriptions of clinical cases, appropriate to the development of theoretical proposition. He extends their application to the understanding of myths whose symbolism can be reapplied, in turn, to the study of the same individual cases. Sometimes he studies individual destinies, using the same clinical experience. We cannot, in fact, be satisfied with the idea that myths and typical dreams have a metaphorical value, valid only within psychoanalysis.

> The elaboration of the clinical material he collected in treatment led him to try to remain faithful to his understanding of the ego, rooted in the body, which sometimes gave rise to a slightly simplistic tendency to a somatopsychic biologism. There, again, we are reminded that the field of psychoanalysis is specific, but that we must not forget the

complexity of the functioning of our body and our nervous system when we allow ourselves some psychoanalytic fantasies in our desire to be creative. (Lebovici, 1978, p. 143)

There is no doubt that, had he lived longer, Abraham, with his tremendous vigour and original thinking, would have played an important part in developing analytic theory and clinical practice. It is my guess that, as heir to Freud's orthodoxy but also a systematic clinician and profound innovator, Abraham would have shaped subsequent analytic thought differently. And, perhaps, the theoretical crisis after Freud's death would have taken another direction altogether had Abraham been alive, a crisis which saw post-Freudian analysts, that is, Anna Freud's followers and Kleinian counterparts, set themselves against each other in what risked opening up a catastrophic split.

Together with depriving the International Psychoanalytical Association of its recognised leader and of its likely successor to Freud, the death of Abraham witnessed the break-up of the most advanced and compact group of fellow psychoanalysts there has ever been.

Freud himself considered Abraham the only colleague who could have succeeded him as leader of the psychoanalytic movement. Abraham's loyalty and independent spirit were assurance enough, no suspicion whatsoever of parricidal intentions having ever arisen, which had, on the other hand, been discovered in the case of Jung and Rank, and suspected even with regard to Ferenczi.

As Aguayo stated (2000), the "succession crisis" following Abraham's death led Freud himself to appoint his daughter Anna as the institutional alter-ego, thus heightening a conflict fraught with consequences between her and London analysts (Jones, Riviere, and Glover in the foreground) who sided with Melanie Klein.

CHAPTER FIVE

The Berlin Psychoanalytic Polyclinic

The first example of its kind, the Psychoanalytic Polyclinic was established specifically to provide analytic treatment to a wide public. The idea in the mind of its founders was that of making treatment accessible to those who would never have been able to afford it, and its coming to be was thanks to the work of a cohesive group of analysts Abraham had encouraged to collaborate with him.

Testament to the sound running of the Berlin Society was, in fact, the Psychoanalytic Polyclinic, which, in addition to enabling those from the less fortunate social classes to undergo analysis, also provided a good educational and training environment for young analysts.

At its helm were Max Eitingon and Ernst Simmel, both also fulfilling the role of supervisors. Underpinning this initiative was the enthusiasm of many Berlin colleagues who saw psychoanalysis as an effective, revolutionary therapy and held that it was the task of the clinic to provide a public service that met demand for treatment, a right that could no longer be denied. The Polyclinic project was brought to fruition in 1920, shortly after a war whose effects had been disastrous for Germany, the nation's economy having collapsed and its healthcare institutions destroyed.

The new clinic could not, however, be created outside the state system, then in a grave crisis and still governed by the leaders of the old political order. Several young psychoanalysts, motivated by the ideal of promoting psychological wellbeing through the efficacy of this new treatment, accepted to work for a modest sum, if not for free. Private contributions and the partly paid work of pupils from the Berlin Institute kept the Polyclinic up and running.

A difficult problem to solve was how to provide sufficient time for all those who applied for psychoanalysis, which, as foreseen from the very start, was an excessively high number. The medical staff, Dr Horney and Dr Klein being among its first members, could offer their combined analytic services for a total of only fourteen hours per day, and renounced any form of publicity from very early on in order to reduce overcrowding. An attempt was made to economise on time by limiting the session to thirty minutes, but this was immediately abandoned. At a later stage, with seven analysts working simultaneously for a total of approximately thirty hours daily, training candidates' hours being on top of this, demand still far exceeded supply. In addition, before long, the five rooms the clinic provided were insufficient to accommodate the analysts and their patients.

Initially, the Polyclinic dealt with desperate cases, such as chronic neuroses that were difficult to treat, and sometimes even physical illnesses, but a gradual, spontaneous selection of more strictly analytical cases soon followed. The gap between demand and the numbers the clinic could actually manage remained an ongoing problem, and no guaranteed criterion for assigning priority really emerged.

Patients from all social classes attended the Polyclinic for treatment: labourers, artisans, teachers, clerks, and professionals, all together in the same waiting room until it was time for their session. Cost depended on what could be afforded, the patient himself being part of this decision-making process, and frequently treatment was free of charge. Naturally, what the patient declared was taken on trust.

The Polyclinic's medical records contained a wide range of conditions: alongside strictly neurotic cases were paranoid states, cyclothymia, and patients suffering from dementia praecox. That there were psychotic cases, despite their small number, is testament to the belief of the Berlin psychoanalysts that all forms of mental disorder could be treated psychoanalytically.

Treatment lasted anything between two or three months and a couple of years, or more. Few cases ended in complete "recovery", the majority benefited from improvement, and several remained unchanged. The analysand was seen between three and five times per week, depending on his needs, and a sort of partitioned analysis was also possible whereby treatment was stopped when there was a marked improvement and could be resumed at a later date.

The Polyclinic's second purpose was that of training analysts according to a "hands-on" approach. Many pupils actually began their training by taking on a patient at the Polyclinic. For the very first time, those wishing to become analysts had to take a course in analytic theory, the cycle of tutorials not being particularly long, only a year and a half at the very most. The basic concept that guided the Berlin training group was that no one could become an analyst unless he had undergone personal analysis, admission to lessons resting on this condition. The one or two cases that the students of the Berlin Institute took on, selected for them by the medical team, were supervised on a regular basis by expert or senior analysts. The pupil would take the notes he had written down after the session to the expert analyst, who would advise on the therapeutic approach to adopt and point out any mistakes or misunderstandings. For the first time, the patient was protected against the beginner's very understandable inexperience, and pupils were given the opportunity to learn within the real interaction of the analytic relationship.

Thus was the psychoanalytic training model outlined. The experience of emotionally understanding oneself through personal analysis was fundamental; then came learning via the clinical supervision of sessions with the patient.

In all Societies of the International Psychoanalytical Association, founded by Freud, personal analysis, clinical supervision, and attending seminars at the training institute are, to the present day, the three pillars for admission to the psychoanalytic profession.

What Abraham could not have understood . . .

The correspondence between Freud and Abraham highlights not only the rich contribution Abraham made to the corpus of psychoanalysis, but it also brings out an area of interest that both shared, that of melancholy, around which a particularly inspiring fellowship began that saw Abraham's contribution being acquired and elaborated by Freud. In mind is "Mourning and melancholia". Perhaps this would not have been written, at least not in the form we know and appreciate it by, without Abraham's careful and patient preparatory work. Theorising on melancholy is the fruit of both minds, but we shall never really know who contributed exactly what.

Abraham dealt with melancholy, or, rather, with manic–depressive insanity, in three important works. The first, "Notes on the psychoanalytical investigation and treatment of manic-depressive insanity and allied conditions", was written in 1911. Here, he discovered for the first time the relationship between mourning, a painful feeling related to a lost object, and melancholy. He sensed the depressed individual's unconscious conflict: besides suffering, self-depreciation and feeling unloved, the core of the depressive pathology contains the patient's inner perception of being unable to love, or, rather, the perception of his own hate and sadism. This unpleasant perception lies at the root of his feeling inadequate and unworthy. There is more, though: if the feeling of guilt is connected to unconscious impulses of hate and revenge, the avowal of guilt then contains fulfilling a wish—that of being a criminal in grand style. Considering himself more guilty than all other human beings, the patient is aroused by his suffering, obtaining pleasure from it. This is why his libido disappears from the rest of the world, and his inability to love, together with his own masochistic tendencies, explain why the melancholic feels impoverished.

On depression in middle age, Abraham wrote here that seeing how past compensation and defences turned out to be ineffective, to the individual everything seems lost and no room is left for change. Further on, after analysing the maniacal reaction, which he saw as a defence against depressive anxiety, Abraham concluded with words of hope for the psychoanalytic treatment of patients suffering from manic–depressive insanity, young and middle-aged alike: despite their appearing detached from the rest of the world, such individuals can be helped to overcome this obstacle through psychoanalysis, and psycho-analysis only. He stressed, too, the benefit of beginning treatment during free intervals. It was legitimate, therefore, to see psychoanaly-sis as freeing psychiatry from the nightmare of therapeutic nihilism.

Freud's reply to Abraham's work was measured and circumspect. In a letter dated 2nd May, 1912, he mentioned Federn's criticism of the work, but added enigmatically, ". . . and then all sorts of things dawned on me which may lead further. We are still only at the begin-nings in that respect" (Falzeder, 2002, p. 151).

Abraham, struck by Freud's answer and allusion, curiously wrote back with a string of questions. He told Freud of a female patient with cyclothymia and asked him about another male patient he had described in his paper and who, unfortunately, had suffered a relapse . . . "You hint that a thing or two dawned on you. I should be very grateful for any suggestions, as I would very much like to give this pitiable patient another try" (Falzeder, 2002, p. 153).

Freud, at the beginning of his letter, kept up his terse style:

> In cyclothymic cases you should just go on digging; one can see more the next time. The difficulty lies not in finding the material but in link-ing up what has been found and grouping it according to its layers. (Falzeder, 2002, p. 154)

Becoming a little more forthcoming, he then added,

> Yet, I have also got the impression from your paper, which I value so
> highly, that the formula is not assured and the elements not yet
> convincingly linked. If I knew any more than you, I should not with-
> hold it from you, but you will learn more from the cases themselves.
> (Falzeder, 2002, p. 154)

After this letter, their dialogue on melancholy seems to end. Other
important matters took centre stage: the break with Jung, the approaching world war, and Abraham's departure for the front as a military
surgeon. In the meantime, Freud enjoyed a period of exceptional
creativity which materialised in his writing twelve essays, "Essays in
preparation of a metapsychology", of which only five were published.

His bond with Abraham as a source of inspiration continued: "I
think of you a great deal, because I am writing on the 'Narcissism'"
(Falzeder, 2002, p. 218).

The following year, melancholy returned to the fore with force
when Freud announced to Abraham in his letter of 18th February 1915
that he had written an essay entitled "Mourning and melancholia". It
was a draft, the final version of which was written up between April
and May of that same year and published two years later in 1917.

At the beginning of 1916, Abraham himself finished another paper
that helped clarify the theoretical base to understanding melancholy:
"The first pregenital stage of the libido". The two works in question
were written almost at the same time, Abraham having taken a year
to produce his final draft, Freud, in his usual manner, having written
his up practically in one go.

In his work, Abraham postulated that melancholy is placed at a
very primitive level. Towards his object, the depressed individual feels
an unconscious desire to swallow him up, annihilate, devour him.
Abraham explained refusing food as a form of self-punishment for
cannibalistic desires. The melancholic's accusations are correlated to,
and keep at bay, cannibalistic desires that induce him to punish
himself by starving to death. Although important from a theoretical
viewpoint, this piece of writing ended up being eclipsed and
surpassed by the forceful *entrée* of "Mourning and melancholia".

Abraham, too, seemed to realise this, writing at the end of his
paper that he had

attempted only to explain the wish-content of certain depressive delusional ideas and the unconscious strivings that underlie certain characteristics in the conduct of the melancholic, and not the causes of
melancholic depression in general. To attempt to solve this far-reach-
ing problem does not come within the scope of the present investigation. (Abraham, 1927[1916], p. 278)

At the end of February 1915, immediately upon receiving the
manuscript of "Mourning and melancholia", Abraham replied to
Freud with a letter that was too measured and distant in tone, betray-
ing his clear disapproval. He wrote that he had nothing to object to in
Freud's work on melancholy, from start to finish, and that what was
written, more clearly and thoroughly, corresponded to his own past
experiences; therefore, for the very first time, one of Freud's works did
not bring anything new or compel him to revise his own ideas. And
so, the subject seemed settled.

Approximately one month later, though, in a letter dated 31st
March 1915, having overcome his reticence, Abraham brought the
matter to the surface once more. This letter, together with Freud's that
followed, are extremely important, as they let us see the careful and
accurate weave of Abraham's preparatory work on depression, and
the major breakthrough in psychoanalytic theory made by Freud.
Abraham acknowledged here that initially it had been difficult for
him to reply to Freud, fearing that he would not have been objective,
having written an essay on the same subject himself.

Freud, in his essay, set out the similarities and differences between
mourning and melancholy: both feature painful dejection and a lack
of interest in the world, but whereas mourning is a painful emotion
connected to the loss of a love object, melancholy is a pathological
state where an inability to love and self-abasement occur, manifesting
as self-reproaches and self-reviling. He stated that, in mourning, nothing about the loss is unconscious, whereas, in melancholy, the object
loss is withdrawn from consciousness. The patient does not know
what he has lost and often ignores the nature of his pain.

In mourning, the world is impoverished and void, in melancholy,
the ego is impoverished and void. The patient continually criticises
himself and, in so doing, seems to sense the truth about himself most
acutely. This is where the difference lies, as the analogy with mourning gives the impression that the melancholic has suffered the loss of

an object, but, when listening to the patient, the impression one gains is that the loss actually concerns his own ego.

Abraham reminded Freud that it was he who had first contra-distinguished melancholic depression and mourning, tracing the roots of depression to the patient's perception of being incapable of loving. He called to mind, too, that he was also the one who had highlighted sadism rather than anal erotism, thus differentiating depression from obsessional neurosis. In melancholy, self-reproaches are nothing other than the expression of deep repressed hostility, plainly evident from the way melancholic patients torment the people who come to their aid, the analyst included. After all, as Freud had observed, such patients are far from coming across as meek, as one might expect from someone claiming to be worthless.

Further on in the letter, Abraham touched upon the most impor-tant, but also the least clear, point that Freud had made: who are the melancholic patient's self-reproaches actually directed against? In a short passage of "Mourning and melancholia", Freud concisely and extremely evocatively expressed various important theoretical concepts that make reference to all his extraordinary work in his essay on narcissism. These new ideas were, however, incomprehensible to Abraham, who confessed to not having understood them.

Freud, in "Mourning and melancholia", advanced the idea that the melancholic, more than attacking himself, is really attacking his own love object. Self-reproaches are, in fact, directed against the love object, from which, however, they are moved away and redirected to the ego: these explicit self-reproaches serve to mask the others, that is, those directed against the love object. It seems that Abraham did not find this point so clear.

Even more complex is Freud's hypothesis that the introjected love object enters the patient's ego. In those twenty or so lines of "Mourn-ing and melancholia", Freud wrote that, in distancing itself from the object, the ego takes away with it part of the lost object. The object loss is, therefore, transformed into an ego loss, and the conflict between the critical activity of the ego and the ego, which identifies with the love object, alters the ego itself.

Freud suggested, too, that the melancholic patient's object choice was not a happy one: "An object-choice . . . had at one time existed; then, owing to a real slight or disappointment coming from this loved person, the object relationship was shattered" (Freud, 1917c, p. 249).

This shattering of the relationship is introjected and remains inside the ego. Via the affective trauma, the patient becomes tied to the frustrating primary object, never to detach himself from it. So, the melancholic introjects the frustrating object, identifies with it, and treats it as if it were part of the self. An unhappy cohabitation! Just as the ego torments the interiorised object for being incapable of loving him, so, too, is the ego itself criticised by the object as unworthy of love. In Freud's words, "Thus the shadow of the object fell upon the ego, and the latter could henceforth be judged by a special agency, as though it were an object, the forsaken object" (Freud, 1917c, p. 249).

The "special agency" Freud writes of in "On narcissism" (1914c) is the superego, at that time not defined as such but as the ego-ideal, that is, the agency that originates out of a narcissistic relationship.

In another passage in "Mourning and melancholia", Freud underlined the narcissistic relationship between the melancholic patient and his object. Embarrassed by Freud's tumultuous development and concentration of ideas, Abraham mentioned in the letter a concept that was dear to him personally: the incorporation of the object as a primitive act of devouring love. He maintained that the importance of the oral zone in melancholy can explain the patient's fear of starving to death, or, conversely, his refusal of food. Here, he alluded to the purely psychotic clinical aspects, such as the loss of differentiation between aggressive and love impulses, identification with a thoroughly bad object, and the system of delusional guilt.

From the letter, one understands, however, that Abraham wrote to Freud of his own contribution without being able to follow and comment on several of his professor's more important ideas. Freud, was, in fact, much further ahead in his theory, given his reference to an internal world and an internal relation in which different objects that are mixed and, at times, mixed up with the Self live alongside and fight against one another, a concept that was foreign to Abraham's theorising. Beginning to loom in this internal world is the superego, the critical agency, the internal object that torments the patient and which, in turn, the patient hates.

Above all, Freud expounded a complex idea concerning the frustration over, and introjection of, the infantile trauma, one that leaves a permanent wound which will flare up at each subsequent frustration or abandonment. Moreover, he indicated that the permanent incorporation of a bad object, or, rather, a melancholic internal object, is the unfortunate outcome of the relation with the primary object, an outcome that will not suitably come to the patient's aid for the rest of his life. The trauma is not something missing or absent, but very present in the form of this bad object.

Freud's theoretical perspective escaped Abraham here, who, at that time, adhered to the concept of phases of libidinal organisation and the nature of the object relation, not that of an inner world with internal objects, such as the superego.

Working on "Mourning and melancholia" in that period, Freud did not answer Abraham's letter until just over one month later, an unusually long time that was not justified by the war. Writing that he had, at that point, finished his essay, he told Abraham how valuable his observations on melancholy had been and how he unhesitatingly drew on and incorporated them in his final draft. In particular, he used the observations on the oral organisation of melancholy, this time, though, not forgetting to mention that it was Abraham who first made the link between mourning and melancholy.[24]

Freud wrote this letter a quarter of an hour after finishing the final draft of "Mourning and melancholia". Clearer acknowledgement of Abraham's contribution to the paper he could not have granted. This was a time of great satisfaction for Freud, aware that considerable progress had been made in psychoanalytic theory. He joked about the fact that he would be fifty-nine years old by the time Abraham received his letter, and, therefore, had every right to retire, but added that it would be better to keep on working in order to leave something for those who will follow them . . .

Among "those who will follow" was Melanie Klein, one of Abraham's young pupils, who indeed went on to further understanding on depression. It was she of whom Abraham wrote to Freud eight years later in a letter dated 7th October 1923, the year in which he completed his third and final work on melancholy: "A short study of the development of the libido, viewed in the light of mental disorders" (1924). It was only at this point that Abraham fully understood and acknowledged the value of his professor's insight.

Freud, Abraham said, had made a crucial step forward when he showed that, upon losing his love object, the melancholic takes it inside via incorporation, the self-reproaches, therefore, being directed against the lost object. But Abraham claimed as his the merit for having brought to light that the melancholic regresses to a very early cannibalistic oral stage. In cannibalism, there is no concern for the object, and neither are there any qualms about exploiting and destroying it. These two processes, accusations against the love object and regression to a primitive cannibalistic phase, are homogeneous and occur together.

In this last paper by Abraham, he claimed that the melancholic's most serious problem is that of harbouring dead objects and trying to understand how to reanimate them. He set out two ways of incorporating, one in normal mourning, the other in pathological mourning: in the former, the object is incorporated in order to internally re-establish the loved person separately; in the latter, incorporation occurs through a movement of expulsion, mortification, and the reintrojection of the love object, the individual therefore identifying with, but not separating from, the object.

Abraham's insight into the oral, cannibalistic, and possessive character of the melancholic's object relation paved the way for an understanding of mourning from other important angles. What he understood was that we want to own the object and we unconsciously believe that separation should not come about. Only, however, if we allow the loved and lost person to separate from us, if we can appreciate him internally without attacking, belittling, or destroying him because of the loss he has caused us through disappearing or dying, can the mourning process be carried through. Only when we become aware that our love object is separate from us, and we grant it a status of freedom and independence, does mourning come to an end.

The exact way in which the work of mourning is carried through, Abraham observed, remained an outstanding problem, yet to be fully understood. Freud, too, in "Mourning and melancholia", left the question unresolved. It was to be Abraham's young and promising pupil, Klein, about whom Abraham enthusiastically wrote to Freud, that, ten years later, would write two important clinical papers on melancholy and structure most of her contribution to psychoanalysis around the theme of mourning and reparation.

In the same letter, Abraham wrote to Freud that the illness of a three-year-old boy his pupil was treating confirmed his idea of the existence of primary melancholy (*Ur-Melancholie*), an early melancholic phase present in the very first stages of development.

Ten years later, at the International Congress in Lucerne, 1934, Melanie Klein carried forward this insight afforded by Abraham. In

"A contribution to the psychogenesis of manic–depressive states", she described the vicissitudes of melancholic object relations and, amid some controversy, postulated a melancholic phase in early infancy. It was Abraham, however, who had sown the seed.

NOTES

1. This is certainly in reference to Sàndor Ferenczi.
2. Abraham wanted the operation to be scheduled according to calculations made by Fleiss, an old friend of Freud's, who collaborated with Abraham professionally. When Abraham wrote to Freud of his decision, together with kind greetings from Fleiss, a former privileged interlocutor of Freud's during his period of scientific solitude and revolutionary intuitions, Freud replied, "This expression of sympathy after twenty years leaves me rather cold!" (Jones, 1953–1957, *Volume 3*, p. 116), a sign that the wound suffered many years earlier still caused him pain.
3. This good relationship with his father inspired Abraham's friendship with Freud. A common Jewish background and a kind of "Talmudic" style of reasoning brought Abraham closer to his Viennese professor, who recognised a special kind of affinity towards him. In comparing him with Jung, Freud wrote to Abraham in 1908, "*you are closer to my intellectual constitution through racial kinship*" (Falzeder, 2002, p. 38, my italics)
4. Jones wrote that Abraham, at the Congress in The Hague in 1920, amazed everyone with an improvised opening speech in Latin after Freud, just one hour earlier, had warned him against speaking German so as not to hurt nationalistic feelings. Besides German,

Abraham was able to speak English, Spanish, Italian, and Rhaeto-Romance (Ladin). He could conduct analysis in English and in Spanish, and had a good knowledge of Danish, Dutch, and French.

5. Abraham wrote the following to Freud in 1907: "The Berlin colleagues I know well. I was a physician at the Berlin mental hospital Dalldorf for more than three years, until I could bear it no longer" (Falzeder, 2002, p. 10).

6. Eitingon would later found the Israel Psychoanalytic Society.

7. Besides Freud, the other members of the Committee were Jones, Abraham, Rank, Ferenczi, Sachs, and, later, Eitingon. Membership implied strict psychoanalytical observance and required any member wishing to dissent from any of the principles of psychoanalytic theory, that is, the unconscious, repression, and infantile sexuality, to do so publicly only after having discussed the matter with the rest of the group.

8. On discovering that his wife's cousin is returning from India, Mathias, a professor of chemistry, falls into depression. His nights are filled with nightmares and he feels the urge to stab his wife with a dagger. After taking refuge at his mother's, he decides to see a psychoanalyst who, being able to recognise the unconscious forces that are controlling his soul, cures him of violent jealousy that has disturbed him since childhood.

    In the programme that accompanies the film, Karl Abraham and Hanns Sachs explained that the numerous problems involved in psychoanalysis could not be described in one film and that many issues had to be omitted as they would have been too difficult for the general public to understand or unsuited to being shown on film.

    Paolo Mereghetti, in his *Dizionario dei film* (Dictionary of Films) (2017), wrote that the film was still interesting today for the way in which it used cinema as a tool to realistically show the "mysteries" of a soul (in fact, the film is rich in detail, the understanding of which is left to the viewer's intuition and keen eye); it being a silent film and talking being central to treatment, together with a rather artificial ending (the main character is happily fishing, and his wife nursing a baby), plays down the incisiveness of that attraction–repulsion men show towards women that is typical of Pabst's works and which is, in fact, the core of the film.

9. These two short essays contain several important elements. The first is the early flight into sexuality (which Melanie Klein would then connect to defences against anxiety) and the second is withdrawal into sexuality in some psychotic states (autoerotism). In addition,

Abraham introduced, albeit in embryonic form, the problem of unconscious guilt and the dissociation of the trauma in cases of sexual abuse.

10. Abraham was among the first to coherently sustain and document that severely ill patients could benefit from psychoanalytic treatment; in this he was followed by Melanie Klein, who carried forward psychoanalytic investigation into primitive mental states and severe pathologies through her treatment of seriously ill children.

11. This paper, which introduced important concepts on melancholy, was published several months after "Mourning and melancholia". Here, Freud made a major contribution to this subject, one that particularly interested Abraham.

12. This sequence clearly shows the theoretical beginnings of the process of reparation that went on to be the kernel of Kleinian theory.

13. Melanie Klein saw progression as going from the partial to the total object: from the breast as part of the mother's body, to the mother perceived as a whole person.

14. The early superego as described by Melanie Klein has its roots in primitive persecutory anxiety based on expecting punishment. Until guilt for the damage caused to the object is mitigated through reparation, anxiety will always signal the threat of the superego.

15. Through the role played by envy, Abraham anticipated several fundamental Kleinian and post-Kleinian themes on development: for example, the importance of envy in producing mental illnesses, the attack on dependency, and the theory of destructive narcissism, all of which prevent the perception of separateness and eliminate the possibility of learning from emotional experience.

16. Following what Freud had sought to do in his study of Leonardo da Vinci (1910c), Abraham cast light on early childhood relations and adolescent emancipation in his works dedicated to Segantini and the Egyptian pharaoh Amenhotep, respectively.

17. This work by Abraham seems (Jones, 1953–1957; Lebovici, 1978) to have led to disagreement between Freud and Jung. In November 1912, during a long walk in Munich, both seemed on the point of bridging the gap that had opened up between them. After lunch, which had brought the most prominent figures of the movement together, Freud once more took up the subject of Abraham's work on Amenhotep to claim that monotheistic religion had its roots in the young pharaoh's Oedipus conflict. Jung vehemently attacked Freud's theory, sustaining that monotheistic religion was known to have come into being for very different reasons. Freud responded just as

argumentatively, then felt unwell, exactly as had happened three years earlier in Bremen when discussing with Jung the son's death wishes towards the father.

18. According to Abraham, alongside the mythical figure Narcissus, who died hypnotised by his own reflection in the water, there is another version of the myth in which Narcissus exchanges his reflection for that of his dead twin sister. Whereas, for Freud, the concept of secondary narcissism as a means of restoring self-love is predominant, for Abraham, emphasis is placed on hostility towards the object.

19. In an amusing exchange between Freud and Abraham in their correspondence, both held that Bleuler had taken the term autism, a basic symptom of schizophrenia, from the psychoanalytic concept of auto-erotism, stripping it, however, of its sexual meaning and, thus, sweetening the psychoanalytic aetiological hypothesis.

20. Castiello d'Antonio (1981, p. 170) stated:

> With his 1911 contribution, he was the one who effectively introduced the study of manic–depressive psychosis to the area of psychoanalytic investigation. If we think for a moment about the essay presented at the First International Psychoanalytic Congress (on the difference between hysteria and dementia praecox) we may grant credit to Abraham not only for having begun investigation into cyclothymia, but also, more generally, for having been one of the first to have shown an interest in the problem of the psychoses from an empirical point of view. (Translated for this edition)

21. In a letter to Freud in 1920, where he set out the characteristics of his new Polyclinic, he wrote: ". . . there is a project to start a special department for the treatment of nervous *children*. I should like to train a woman doctor particularly for this" (Falzeder, 2002, p. 418).

22. Klein's *The Psychoanalysis of Children* (1932) carries this dedication: "To the memory of Karl Abraham in gratitude and admiration".

23. At a later date, Klein completed her description of this complex process, that is, projective identification, where the oral and possessive character in the relation with the object is maintained. She differentiated it from introjective identification, in which taking inside occurs through separation and gratitude.

24. It is quite interesting to note here that it was, in fact, Freud who had first made a link between mourning and melancholy in "Draft G" (1895).

REFERENCES

Abraham, H. (1974). *Karl Abraham. An Unfinished Biography*. New York: Grant Allan.

Abraham, K. (1907a). On the significance of sexual trauma in childhood for the symptomatology of dementia praecox. In: *Clinical Papers and Essays on Psychoanalysis* (pp. 13–20). London: Hogarth Press, 1955.

Abraham, K. (1907b). The experiencing of sexual trauma as a form of sexual activity. In: *Selected Papers on Psychoanalysis* (pp. 47–63). London: Hogarth Press, 1927.

Abraham, K. (1908). The psychosexual differences between hysteria and dementia praecox. In: *Selected Papers on Psychoanalysis* (pp. 64–79). London: Hogarth Press, 1927.

Abraham, K. (1911a). Giovanni Segantini: a psycho-analytical study. In: *Clinical Papers and Essays on Psychoanalysis* (pp. 210–261). London: Hogarth Press, 1955.

Abraham, K. (1911b). Notes on the psycho-analytical investigation and treatment of manic–depressive insanity and allied conditions. In: *Selected Papers on Psychoanalysis* (pp. 137–156). London: Hogarth Press, 1927.

Abraham, K. (1912). Amenhotep IV. Psycho-analytical contributions towards the understanding of his personality and of the monotheistic cult of Aton. In: *Clinical Papers and Essays on Psychoanalysis* (pp. 262–290). London: Hogarth Press, 1955.

Abraham, K. (1916). The first pregenital stage of the libido. In: *Selected Papers on Psychoanalysis* (pp. 248–279). London: Hogarth Press, 1927.

Abraham, K. (1917). Ejaculatio praecox. In: *Selected Papers on Psychoanalysis* (pp. 280–298). London: Hogarth Press, 1927.

Abraham, K. (1919a). A particular form of neurotic resistance against the psycho-analytic method. In: *Selected Papers on Psychoanalysis* (pp. 303–311). London: Hogarth Press, 1927.

Abraham, K. (1919b). The applicability of psycho-analytic treatment to patients at an advanced age. In: *Selected Papers on Psychoanalysis* (pp. 312–317). London: Hogarth Press, 1927.

Abraham, K. (1920). Manifestations of the female castration complex. In: *Selected Papers on Psychoanalysis* (pp. 338–369). London: Hogarth Press, 1927.

Abraham, K. (1921–1925). Psycho-analytical studies on character-formation. In: *Selected Papers on Psychoanalysis* (pp. 370–406). London: Hogarth Press, 1927.

Abraham, K. (1924). A short study of the development of the libido, viewed in the light of mental disorders. In: *Selected Papers on Psychoanalysis* (pp. 418–501). London: Hogarth Press, 1927.

Aguayo, J. (2000). Patronage in the dispute over child analysis between Melanie Klein and Anna Freud. *International Journal of Psychoanalysis, 81*: 733–753.

Barale, F., & Ucelli, S. (2001). Alle fonti delle concezioni psicodinamiche delle psicosi: Karl Abraham e la psichiatria del suo tempo. *Rivista di Psicoanalisi, XLVII*(4): 693–709.

Bleuler, E. (1911). *Dementia Praecox or the Group of Schizophrenias*. New York: International Universities Press, 1950.

Britton, R. (2000). What part does narcissism play in narcissistic disorders? Paper presented to the Herbert Rosenfeld Conference, London 8 April (unpublished).

Castiello d'Antonio, A. (1981). *Karl Abraham e la psicoanalisi clinica*. Rome: Bulzoni.

Cremerius, J. (1969–1971). Introduction to Karl Abraham's collected works. In: Karl Abraham *Opere* (pp. 9–33). Turin: Boringhieri.

Falzeder, E. (Ed.) (2002). *The Complete Correspondence of Sigmund Freud and Karl Abraham 1907–1925 Completed Edition*. London: Karnac.

Fenichel, O. (1945). *The Psychoanalytic Theory of Neurosis*. New York: W. W. Norton.

Freud, S. (1901b). *The Psychopathology of Everyday Life*. S. E., 6. London: Hogarth Press.

Freud, S. (1905d). *Three Essays on the Theory of Sexuality. S. E., 7*: 125–245. London: Hogarth Press.

Freud, S. (1910c). *Leonardo da Vinci and a Memory of His Childhood. S. E., 11*: 59–137. London: Hogarth Press.

Freud, S. (1911c). *Psycho-analytic Notes upon an Autobiographical Account of a Case of Paranoia. S. E., 12*: 3–82. London: Hogarth Press.

Freud, S. (1912–1913). *Totem and Taboo. S. E., 13*: 1–161. London: Hogarth Press.

Freud, S. (1914c). On narcissism: an introduction. *S. E., 14*: 67–102. London: Hogarth Press.

Freud, S. (1915c). Instincts and their vicissitudes. *S. E., 14*: 111–140. London: Hogarth Press.

Freud, S. (1917e). Mourning and melancholia. *S. E., 14*: 239–258. London: Hogarth Press.

Freud, S. (1920). *A General Introduction to Psychoanalysis*. New York: Horace Liveright.

Freud, S. (1920g). *Beyond the Pleasure Principle. S. E., 18*: 7–64. London: Hogarth Press.

Freud, S., & Pfister, O. (1963). *Psychoanalysis and Faith: Letters of Sigmund Freud and Oskar Pfister*. New York: Basic Books.

Glover, E. (1928). Selected Papers of Karl Abraham with an Introductory Memoir by Ernest Jones. *International Journal of Psychoanalysis, 9*: 120–124.

Good, M. (1995). Karl Abraham, Sigmund Freud and the fate of seduction theory. *Journal of the American Psychoanalytic Association, 43*: 1137–1167.

Horney, K. (1936). The problem of the negative therapeutic reaction. *Psychoanalysis Quarterly, 5*: 29–44.

Jones, E. (1926). Karl Abraham 1877–1925. *International Journal of Psychoanalysis, 7*: 155–181.

Jones, E. (1953–1957). *The Life and Work of Sigmund Freud (3 volumes)*. New York: Basic Books.

Jung, C. G. (1911). Symbols of transformation. In: *C. W., 5*. Princeton, NJ: Princeton University Press, 1956.

Kerr, J. (1993). *A Most Dangerous Method*. New York: Alfredo Knopf.

Klein, M. (1932). *The Psychoanalysis of Children*. London: Hogarth Press.

Klein, M. (1935). A contribution to the psychogenesis of manic–depressive states. *International Journal of Psychoanalysis, 16*: 145–174.

Klein, M. (1940). Mourning and its relation to manic–depressive states. *International Journal of Psychoanalysis, 21*: 125–153.

Klein, M. (1957). *Envy and Gratitude and Other Works 1946–1963*. London: Hogarth Press, 1975.

Le Rider, J. (1982). La psychanalyse en Allemagne. In: Roland Jaccard, *Histoire de la psychanalyse, Volume 2* (pp. 107–143). Paris: Hachette.

Lebovici, S. (1978). Presidential Address in honour of the centenary of the birth of Karl Abraham. *International Journal of Psychoanalysis, 59*: 133–144.

May, U. (2001). Abraham's discovery of the 'bad' mother. A contribution to the history of the theory of depression. *International Journal of Psychoanalysis, 82*: 283–305.

McGuire, W. (Ed.) (1974). *The Freud/Jung Letters*. London: Hogarth Press and Routledge and Kegan Paul.

Mereghetti, P. (2017). *Dizionario dei film*. Milan: Baldini & Castaldi.

Paskauskas, R. A. (Ed.) (1993). *The Complete Correspondence of Sigmund Freud and Ernest Jones 1908–1939*. Cambridge, MA: Harvard University Press.

Rank, O. (1929). *The Trauma of Birth*. London: Routledge, 1999.

Riviere, J. (1936). A contribution to the analysis of the negative therapeutic reaction. *International Journal of Psychoanalysis, 17*: 304–320.

Rosenfeld, H. (1971). A clinical approach to the psychoanalytic theory of the life and death instincts: an investigation into the aggressive aspects of narcissism. *International Journal of Psychoanalysis, 52*: 169–178.

Sachs, H. (1926). Gedenkreden über K. Abraham. *International Zeitschrift für Psychoanalyse, 2*: 198–202.

Steiner, J. (1987). The interplay between pathological organizations and the paranoid–schizoid and depressive positions. *International Journal of Psychoanalysis, 70*: 611–616.

INDEX

Printed in the United States
by Baker & Taylor Publisher Services